to circ

42

W9-BTT-771

American
Civil Rights
Primary Sources

American Civil Rights Primary Sources

Phillis Engelbert

Betz Des Chenes, Editor

AN IMPRINT OF THE GALE GROUP

DETROIT · SAN FRANCISCO · LONDON
BOSTON · WOODBRIDGE, CT

Phillis Engelbert

Staff

Elizabeth Des Chenes, *U•X•L Senior Editor*
Carol DeKane Nagel, *U•X•L Managing Editor*
Thomas L. Romig, *U•X•L Publisher*

Shalice Shah-Caldwell, *Permissions Associate (Pictures)*

Rita Wimberley, *Senior Buyer*
Evi Seoud, *Assistant Production Manager*
Dorothy Maki, *Manufacturing Manager*

Pamela A. E. Galbreath, *Senior Art Director*
Cynthia Baldwin, *Product Design Manager*

LM Design, *Typesetting*

Library of Congress Cataloging-in-Publication Data

American civil rights: primary sources/ [compiled by] Phillis Engelbert; edited by Betz Des Chenes.

p.cm.

Includes bibliographical references and index.

Summary: Includes over fifteen documents, including speeches, autobiographical text, and proclamations, related to the civil rights movement, and arranged in the categories of economic rights, desegregation, and human rights.

ISBN 0-7876-3170-1.

I. Monorities—civil rights—United States—History Sources Juvenile literature. 2. Civil rights movements—United States— History Sources Juvenile literature. 3. United States—Race relations Sources Juvenile literature. 4. United States—Ethnic relations Sources Juvenile literature. [1. Civil rights movements. 2. Race relations Sources.] I. Des Chenes, Betz. II. Engelbert, Phillis. III. Des Chenes, Betz.

E184. A1A56 1999
305. 8' 00973—dc21

Contents

Daisy Bates.
*Reproduced by permission of
AP/Wide World Photos.*

Native Americans at a rally
for fishing rights.
*Reproduced by permission of
AP/Wide World Photos.*

John F. Kennedy.
*Reproduced by permission of
the Library of Congress.*

Advisory Board

Special thanks are due for the invaluable comments and suggestions provided by U•X•L's American Civil Rights Reference Library advisors:

- Eduardo Bonilla-Silva, Professor of Sociology, Texas A&M University, College Station, Texas

- Frances Hasso, Assistant Professor of Sociology, Antioch College, Yellow Springs, Ohio

- Annalissa Herbert, Graduate student, American Culture program, University of Michigan, Ann Arbor, Michigan

- Patrick R. LeBeau, Assistant Professor of American Thought and Language, Michigan State University, East Lansing, Michigan

- Premilla Nadasen, Assistant Professor of African American History, Queens College, New York City

- Kamal M. Nawash, Esq., Director of Legal Services, American-Arab Anti-Discrimination Committee, Washington, D.C.

- Diane Surati, Teacher, Crossett Brook Middle School, Waterbury, Vermont

- Jan Toth-Chernin, Media Specialist, Greenhills School, Ann Arbor, Michigan

Reader's Guide

A merican Civil Rights: Primary Sources presents 19 excerpted documents written by people who worked to advance the cause of civil rights in the United States. The articles, autobiographical essays, declarations, government documents, poems, and speeches in this volume reflect the experiences of artists, educators, labor organizers, participants, and movement leaders. Some documents, such as Martin Luther King Jr.'s "I Have a Dream" and "Letter from Birmingham City Jail," are readily recognizable, while other selections, such as Rodolfo "Corky" Gonzales's *I Am Joaquín,* have important meaning to certain groups of people (in this case, Mexican Americans), but are relatively unknown to a wider audience.

Format

The excerpts presented in *American Civil Rights : Primary Sources* are organized into three chapters. Each of the chapters focuses on a specific theme: Desegregation, Economic Rights, and Human Rights. Every chapter opens with an historical overview, followed by three to seven document excerpts.

Each excerpt is divided into six sections:

- **Introductory material** places the document and its author in an historical context
- **Things to remember** offers readers important background information about the featured text
- **Excerpt** presents the document in its original spelling and format
- **What happened next...** discusses the impact of the document on both the speaker and his or her audience
- **Did you know...** provides interesting facts about each document and its author
- **Sources** presents references for more information on the documents and the speakers

Additional features

Many of the *American Civil Rights: Primary Sources* entries contain a short boxed biography of the speaker. Other sidebar boxes highlight related people and documents, while over fifty black-and-white photos help illuminate the text. Each excerpt is accompanied by a glossary running alongside the primary document that defines terms, people, and ideas. The volume also includes a timeline, a general "words to know" section, and a cumulative index.

Dedication

These books are dedicated to all the heroic women and men, of all races, who have championed civil rights throughout this nation's history, and to the young people who will work to expand civil rights in the next millennium.

Special Thanks

Special thanks goes to Elizabeth Des Chenes, Senior Developmental Editor at U•X•L, for her support and guidance; to Nancy Dziedzic, for her careful attention to detail; to all members of the advisory board for reading long manuscripts and offering thoughtful suggestions; to James W. Sullivan for providing access to his extensive private library; to Alfonso H. Lozano for answering questions about Mexican history and translating Spanish terms; to the reference librarians at the Ann Arbor Public Library for assistance in locating obscure resources; to William F. Shea for his unique insights; and to Ryan Patrick Shea for his inspiration.

Comments and suggestions

We welcome your comments on this work as well as your suggestions for topics to be featured in future editions of *American Civil Rights: Primary Sources*. Please write: Editors, *American Civil Rights: Primary Sources*, U•X•L, 27500 Drake Rd., Farmington Hills, MI 48331–3535; call toll-free: 1–800–877–4253; fax: 248–414–5043; or send e-mail via www.galegroup.com.

Timeline of Events in the American Civil Rights Movement

1890   The National American Woman Suffrage Association (NAWSA) is formed by the merging of the National Woman Suffrage Association (NWSA) and the American Woman Suffrage Association (AWSA). The NAWSA's goal is to fight for the passage of a constitutional amendment guaranteeing women the right to vote.

1920   The Nineteenth Amendment is passed, granting women the right to vote.

February 19, 1942   President Franklin D. Roosevelt signs Executive Order 9066, authorizing the internment of 120,000 Japanese Americans in camps from 1942 to 1945.

March 20, 1946   The last of the detention camps for Japanese Americans, Tule Lake in California, is closed.

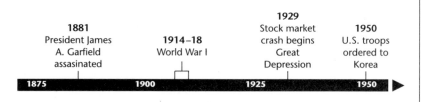

| 1881 President James A. Garfield assasinated | 1914–18 World War I | 1929 Stock market crash begins Great Depression | 1950 U.S. troops ordered to Korea |

1875   1900   1925   1950

Japanese American internees await processing at the Santa Anita Assembly Center in California.
Reproduced by permission of the National Archives and Records Administration.

Malcolm X.
Reproduced by permission of AP/Wide World Photos.

May 17, 1954 In *Brown v. Board of Education of Topeka, Kansas,* the Supreme Court declares school segregation unconstitutional.

January 10 and 11, 1957 The Southern Christian Leadership Conference (SCLC) is founded in Atlanta, Georgia. Martin Luther King Jr. is named president and Ella Baker is hired as acting executive director and office manager.

September 25, 1957 Following two failed attempts earlier in the month, the "Little Rock Nine" successfully integrate Central High School in Little Rock, Arkansas.

April 16–18, 1960 The Student Nonviolent Coordinating Committee (SNCC; pronounced "snick") is founded at a conference organized by Ella Baker in Raleigh, North Carolina.

1961 Civil rights activists conduct Freedom Rides throughout the South, testing the enforcement of Supreme Court rulings outlawing segregated seating on interstate (crossing state lines) buses and trains.

April 1963 Martin Luther King Jr. writes his "Letter from Birmingham City Jail."

August 23, 1963 More than 250,000 people participate in the March on Washington for Jobs and Freedom. Martin Luther King Jr. gives his "I Have a Dream" speech and John Lewis delivers an impassioned address on behalf of the Student Nonviolent Coordinating Committee.

March, 1964 Malcolm X forms a black-nationalist group, the Organization of Afro-American Unity (OAAU).

June–September, 1964 One thousand college student volunteers descend on Mississippi for Freedom Summer. The students register voters, run freedom schools, and organize the Mississippi Freedom Democratic Party (MFDP).

August, 1964 Fannie Lou Hamer testifies on behalf of the Mississippi Freedom Democratic Party before the cre-

1955 British prime minister Winston Churchill resigns	**1957** Soviet Union launches first Earth satellite, Sputnik I	**1959** Alaska and Hawaii admitted to the Union as 49th and 50th states
1954 1956	1958	1960

dentials committee at the Democratic Party national convention in Atlantic City, New Jersey.

1965 The Crusade for Justice, a Chicano-rights organization, is founded by Rodolfo "Corky" Gonzales in Denver, Colorado.

1965 The National Farm Workers Association, which changes its name to the United Farm Workers (UFW) in April 1966, is founded by César Chávez and Dolores Huerta in Delano, California.

February 21, 1965 Malcolm X is assassinated in Harlem, New York.

September 8, 1965 Six hundred Filipino American members of the Agricultural Workers Organizing Committee, led by Philip Vera Cruz, initiate a strike in the grape vineyards of Coachella, California. The strikers are joined two weeks later by the Mexican American workers' National Farm Workers Association (in 1966 the two groups merge to form the United Farm Workers). The strike ends in victory in July 1970.

1967 Rodolfo "Corky" Gonzales writes the epic poem *I am Joaquín*.

April 4, 1968 Martin Luther King Jr. is assassinated in Memphis, Tennessee.

July 1968 The American Indian Movement (AIM) is founded in Minneapolis, Minnesota.

June 27, 1969 The Stonewall Rebellion—a massive demonstration by lesbians and gay men in New York City—is instigated by the police raid of a gay bar in Greenwich Village. The rebellion is considered the start of the gay liberation movement.

February 27–May 8, 1973 Members of the American Indian Movement and other reservation residents occupy the

Dolores Huerta.
Reproduced by permission of AP/Wide World Photos.

Vernon Bellecourt.
Reproduced by permission of Corbis-Bettmann.

1963
President John F. Kennedy is assasinated

1965
First U.S. combat forces land in Vietnam

1967
State laws forbidding interracial marriage declared unconstitutional by the U.S. Supreme Court

1962   1964   1966   1968

Disabled protesters demonstrate against Federal Aviation Administration regulations.
Reproduced by permission of AP/Wide World Photos.

village of Wounded Knee on the Pine Ridge Reservation in South Dakota. The group's action is in protest of the corrupt tribal government of chairman Dick Wilson.

1974 In the landmark court case *United States v. Washington*, Judge George H. Boldt rules that Native Americans in the northwestern United States have the right, established by treaty, to fish free from state interference.

1983 *Personal Justice Denied* is published. This report, issued by the Commission on Wartime Relocation and Internment of Civilians, examined the harm caused by the exclusion, evacuation, and internment of Japanese Americans during World War II.

1988 Congress passes the Civil Liberties Act, thereby authorizing the payment of $20,000 to each Japanese American survivor of the internment camps and issuing an apology to all former detainees.

1990 Congress passes the Americans with Disabilities Act, thereby prohibiting discrimination against people with disabilities in the areas of employment, government-run programs and services, public accommodations, and telecommunications.

1996 President Bill Clinton signs into law the Defense of Marriage Act, thus defining marriage as the union of one man and one woman. Two years later, in separate statewide referenda, voters in Hawaii and Alaska reject same-sex marriage in their states.

May 15, 1999 Judge John Wisdom, the last survivor of the appeals court that forced the Deep South to give up segregation, dies in New Orleans, Louisiana. In the 1960s Wisdom and three fellow members of the Fifth Circuit Court of Appeals issued several rulings that expanded the Supreme Court's mandate of desegregation "with all deliberate speed."

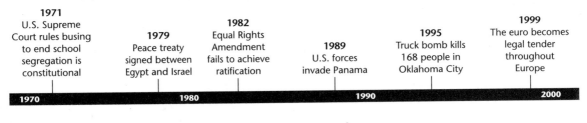

1971
U.S. Supreme Court rules busing to end school segregation is constitutional

1979
Peace treaty signed between Egypt and Israel

1982
Equal Rights Amendment fails to achieve ratification

1989
U.S. forces invade Panama

1995
Truck bomb kills 168 people in Oklahoma City

1999
The euro becomes legal tender throughout Europe

1970   1980   1990   2000

Words to Know

A

Abolitionism: The belief that slavery should be immediately terminated; the social movement to eliminate slavery.

Abolitionist: A person who works for the elimination of slavery.

Affirmative action: A set of federal government policies, primarily in education and employment, that give preferential treatment to racial minorities and women (groups that have historically been victims of discrimination).

Agribusiness: Farming processes—for example, the storage and distribution of produce—operated on large, industrial scale.

Allotment: The U.S. government policy, implemented in the late 1800s and early 1900s, of dividing up reservation lands and parceling them out to individual Native Americans.

American Indian Movement (AIM): The best-known and most militant Native American rights organization of the 1960s and 1970s.

Americans with Disabilities Act (ADA): Federal legislation, passed in 1990, that prohibits discrimination against people with disabilities in the areas of employment, government-run programs and services, public accommodations (such as hotels, restaurants, and movie theaters), and telecommunications.

Anglo: Term used by Hispanic Americans to describe a person of European descent.

Assimilation: The process of becoming like, or being absorbed into, the dominant culture.

B

Black Codes: Laws developed after the Civil War (1861–65) that denied black Americans the right to vote, the right to own property, and the right to pursue employment or otherwise advance their economic status.

Black nationalism: Movement to create political, economic, and social self-sufficiency among black people.

Black Panther Party (BPP): Organization founded in Oakland, California, in 1966 by black activists seeking to stop police abuse and provide social services (including a free breakfast program and a free health clinic). BPP members carried arms in public and came into frequent conflict with the police.

Black power: Social movement and rallying cry of radical black activists in the mid-1960s through mid-1970s. To many African Americans, the slogan stood for racial pride and the belief that blacks held the power to create a better society for themselves.

"Bloody Sunday:" March 7, 1965—the day on which state troopers in Selma, Alabama, viciously beat civil rights demonstrators trying to cross the Edmund Pettus Bridge on their way to Montgomery, Alabama.

Boycott: The refusal to purchase a product or use a service. A boycott gives an oppressed group economic leverage in their struggle for social change.

Brown v. Board of Education of Topeka, Kansas: Supreme Court decision in 1954 that declared school segregation unconstitutional.

C

Chicano: Term used by politically active Mexican Americans to describe themselves; the word symbolized their pride in their cultural heritage.

Civil disobedience: Nonviolent action in which participants refuse to obey certain laws, with the purpose of challenging the fairness of those laws.

Civil Rights Act of 1964: The most expansive civil rights policy in American history, this act outlawed a variety of types of discrimination based on race, color, religion, or national origin.

Communism: A political and social system based on sharing goods equally in the community and owning property collectively.

Congress on Racial Equality (CORE): Civil rights organization formed in 1942 that promoted nonviolent direct action.

Counter-Intelligence Program (COINTELPRO): A Federal Bureau of Investigation (FBI) program whose official purpose was to combat domestic terrorism. In actuality, COINTELPRO was used to weaken the anti-Vietnam War and civil rights movements, the Black Panther Party, AIM, and other militant organizations of people of color.

Crusade for Justice: Chicano-rights and social-service organization, founded in 1965 in Denver, Colorado, that worked to end police brutality and discrimination in the public schools.

D

Desegregation: The elimination of laws and social customs that call for the separation of races.

Disability: A restriction or lack of ability to perform an activity considered part of the range of normal human behaviors.

E

Enfranchisement: The granting of the right to vote.

Executive Order 9066: Decree issued by President Franklin D. Roosevelt in 1942 that led to the internment of 120,000 Japanese Americans in camps during World War II. The first internment camp opened in 1942, and the last camp closed in 1946.

F

Fish-in: A form of civil disobedience in which Indian activists fished in violation of state laws in order to assert their treaty rights. This tactic was frequently used in the 1960s and 1970s in Washington and Oregon.

Freedom Rides: Journeys made throughout the South by integrated groups of people to test the enforcement of a pair of Supreme Court rulings striking down the constitutionality of segregated seating on interstate (crossing state lines) buses and trains.

Freedom Summer: Mississippi civil rights campaign in the summer of 1964, in which about 1,000 northern college student volunteers registered voters and operated educational and social programs.

G

Grandfather clause: A policy that exempted white people from literacy tests to qualify to vote. The clause stated that all people entitled to vote in 1866, as well as their descendants, could vote without taking a literacy test. All descendants of 1866 voters were white, since blacks only gained the constitutional right to vote in 1870.

Great Depression: The worst economic crisis to hit the United States, the Depression began with the stock market crash in 1929 and lasted until 1939.

H

Handicap: A physical or mental condition that prevents or limits a person's ability to lead a normal life.

Hate Crimes Prevention Act (HCPA): Proposed federal legislation that would amend current federal law—which permits federal prosecution of a hate crime based on religion, national origin, or color—to include real or perceived sexual orientation, sex, and disability.

Heterosexuality: Sexual desire or behavior exhibited between persons of opposite sexes.

Highlander Folk School: A civil rights and social justice institute in founded in 1932 in Tennessee. Highlander was unique in the pre-civil rights South because it was a racially integrated facility.

Hispanic American: A person living in the United States who was born in, or whose descendants were born in, a Spanish-speaking country (synonymous with Hispanic or Hispano).

Homosexuality: Sexual desire or behavior exhibited between persons of the same sex.

I

Indian Civil Rights Act: Legislation passed by Congress in 1968 to guarantee the civil rights of American Indians living on reservations.

Indian Removal Act: Legislation signed in 1830 by President Andrew Jackson, mandating the relocation of American Indians living east of the Mississippi River to a tract of land called "Indian Territory" (present-day Oklahoma).

Indian Reorganization Act: Legislation passed in 1934 that put an end to allotment, returned "surplus" reservation lands to the tribes, recognized tribal governments, and recommended that Indian nations adopt their own constitutions.

Integration: The combination of facilities, previously separated by race, into single, multiracial systems.

Internment: The act of being confined against one's will.

Involuntary servitude: Any situation in which a person is made to perform services against her or his will.

J

Jim Crow laws: A network of legislation and customs that dictated the separation of the races on every level of society.

K

Ku Klux Klan: Anti-black terrorist group formed in the South in the aftermath of the Civil War (1861–65) that has for decades intimidated and committed acts of violence against black Americans and members of other racial and ethnic minorities.

L

La Raza Unida: Mexican American political party (pronounced la RAHssa oonEEDa; the name means "The People United") founded in 1969 that embraced bilingual education, the regulation of public utilities, farm subsidies, and tax breaks for low-income people.

Latino: Person living in the United States who was born in, or whose descendants were born in, the geographic region of Latin America.

Literacy test: Selectively administered to black applicants, the test required would-be voters to read and/or interpret a section of the state Constitution to the satisfaction of the registrar.

Lynching: Execution-style murder of a person (usually an African American), often by hanging, by a white mob.

M

Mexican American Legal Defense and Education Fund (MALDEF): Organization formed in 1968 to promote the civil rights of Mexican Americans through the legal system.

Mississippi Freedom Democratic Party (MFDP): Multi-racial political party created in Mississippi in 1964 that served as an alternative to the all-white Democratic Party.

N

Nation of Islam (NOI): Organization of Black Muslims that advocates prayer, self-discipline, separatism, and economic self-help for African American communities.

National American Woman Suffrage Association (NAWSA): Organization, founded in 1890, that fought for the passage of a constitutional amendment guaranteeing women the right to vote.

National Association for the Advancement of Colored People (NAACP): Civil rights organization formed in 1909 that promotes racial equality and the end of racial prejudice.

Nonviolence: The rejection of all forms of violence, even in response to the use of violence by one's adversaries.

O

Organization of Afro-American Unity (OAAU): A black-nationalist group formed by Malcolm X (1925–1965), the OAAU advocated that African Americans practice self-defense, study African history and reclaim African culture, aspire to economic self-sufficiency, and become active in their communities.

P

Passive resistance: The quiet but firm refusal to comply with unjust laws, passive resistance involves putting one's body on the line, risking arrest, and attempting to win over one's foes with morally persuasive arguments.

Personal Justice Denied: Report published in 1983 by the congressionally appointed Commission on Wartime Relocation and Internment of Civilians. The report explored the harm caused by the exclusion, evacuation, and internment of Japanese Americans during World War II (1939–45).

Plessy v. Ferguson: An 1896 Supreme Court decision upholding the constitutionality of the Jim Crow laws. *Plessy* specifically upheld a Louisiana law mandating separate railroad cars for black and white passengers.

Poll tax: A tax that blacks were required to pay in order to vote. Once at the voting booth, voters had to provide proof of that they had paid the tax.

Poor People's March on Washington: Protest march to the nation's capital by poor people of all races, from all parts of the country, in May 1968. The march had been initiated by Martin Luther King Jr. before his death.

R

Radicalization: The process of moving toward drastic, fundamental change.

Reconstruction: The post-Civil War era in which emancipated slaves were granted civil rights and the Southern states reincorporated into the nation.

"Red Power:" American Indian rights movement of the 1960s and 1970s.

Relocation: U.S. government policy, beginning in 1949, by which Native Americans were encouraged to move from reservations and into cities.

Reservation: Tract of land set aside by the U.S. government for use by an Indian tribe.

Roe v. Wade: Landmark 1973 Supreme Court case that resulted in the legalization of abortion throughout the United States.

S

Scabs: Workers hired to take the place of, and weaken the resolve of, striking workers.

Segregation: The separation of the races, as dictated by laws and social customs.

Segregationist: A person who promotes or enforces the separation of the races.

Separatism: The rejection of the dominant culture and institutions, in favor of a separate culture and institutions comprised of one's own minority group.

Sharecropper: Landless farmer who works a plot of land and in return gives the landowner a share of the crop.

Sit-in: Form of civil rights protest in which black students, sometimes joined by white students, requested service at segregated lunch counters and refused to leave when denied service.

Southern Christian Leadership Conference (SCLC): Organization of black ministers, formed in 1957, that coordinated civil rights activities in the South in the 1960s and continues to work for racial justice today.

Southern Manifesto: Denunciation of the Supreme Court's 1954 school desegregation ruling by 101 southern congressional representatives and senators.

Sovereignty: State of being independent and self-governed.

Stereotype: Simple and inaccurate image of the members of a particular racial or ethnic group.

Student Nonviolent Coordinating Committee (SNCC; pronounced "snick"): Student civil rights organization that engaged in voter registration activities and nonviolent protests in the 1960s.

Suffrage: The right to vote in public elections.

Suffragist: A person who works for the right to vote in public elections.

Sweatshop: Factory in which workers are paid low wages and toil in unpleasant and often dangerous conditions.

T

Termination: U.S. government policy in the 1950s of terminating (ending) the standing relationships, governed by treaties, between the United States and Native American tribes.

Trail of Broken Treaties: Protest by the American Indian Movement (AIM) at the Bureau of Indian Affairs (BIA) in Washington, D.C., in the fall of 1972. AIM demanded the restoration of tribes' treaty-making status, the return of stolen Indian lands, and the revocation of state government authority over Indian affairs. AIM demonstrators occupied the BIA building for six days.

Treaty: Agreement between two independent nations, usually defining the benefits to both parties that will result from one side ceding (giving up) its land.

U

United Farm Workers (UFW): Union of farm workers, led by César Chávez, formed in Delano, California, in 1966.

V

Vietnam War: War lasting from 1954 to 1975 in which the United States sided with South Vietnam in the fight against communism in North Vietnam.

Vigilante: Member of a citizens' group that uses extra-legal means to intimidate a certain group of people, for example, foreigners or people of color.

Voting Rights Act: Legislation enacted in 1965 that outlawed all practices used to deny blacks the right to vote and empowered federal registrars to register black voters.

W

White Citizens' Council: Organization of white businessmen and professionals that worked to forestall the political and economic advancement of African Americans in the South from the 1950s through the 1970s.

White primary: Practice adopted by southern states in the late 1800s that excluded blacks from Democratic Party primaries. Since the Democratic Party held a virtual monopoly over political power in the South, the only meaningful votes were cast in the primaries. White primaries effectively denied blacks the right to vote.

White supremacist: A person who believes in the inherent supremacy of the white race above all other races.

Wounded Knee: Tiny village on the Pine Ridge Reservation in South Dakota. In 1890 Wounded Knee was the site of a massacre of between 150 and 370 Indians by U.S.

military forces; in 1973 the village was occupied by members of the American Indian Movement (AIM) and other reservation residents for ten weeks, in protest of the corrupt tribal government of chairman Dick Wilson.

Desegregation

The primary objective of civil rights activists from the mid-1950s through the mid-1960s was desegregation (the elimination of laws and social customs that dictate the separation of the races). The network of legislation and practices that decreed racial segregation on every level of society, called the Jim Crow system, was first imposed in the 1890s. While Jim Crow laws were primarily used to subjugate African Americans throughout the South, they were also used against members of various racial and ethnic minorities in the Southwest and other regions.

The African American civil rights movement fought for desegregation in schools, in public accommodations (including restaurants, hotels, stores, libraries, and swimming pools), in public transportation, and in the political arena (for voting rights). The earliest legal victory for desegregation came in education, with the 1954 Supreme Court decision *Brown v. Board of Education of Topeka, Kansas*. In that ruling the Court unanimously outlawed segregation in public schools, claiming that segregated schools, while separate, were "inherently unequal."

The *Brown* lawsuit was argued by attorneys for the National Association for the Advancement of Colored People (NAACP). One of the most compelling pieces of evidence the NAACP lawyers presented was the research of noted black psychologist **Kenneth B. Clark** (1914–). Clark had conducted interviews with African American schoolchildren using dolls of different skin colors. He found that the majority of the children interviewed showed a preference for the white dolls. Clark observed that the children had poor self-esteem and a negative image of their race. He was able to link the children's psychological damage to their segregated education.

The *Brown* ruling did not bring about the immediate desegregation of public schools. School officials, lawmakers at every level of government, and groups of white citizens throughout the South condemned the ruling and refused to follow its mandate. School desegregation only came about gradually, through the courageous efforts of black schoolchildren and civil rights activists. In some parts of the South it took up to fifteen years after the *Brown* decision for desegregation to occur.

In some locations, mobs of hostile white citizens and law enforcement officials attempted to physically block black students from entering "white" schools. Such was the case in Little Rock, Arkansas, in September 1957, when nine African American students tried to integrate Central High School. The students, assisted by **Daisy Bates** (1920–), president of the Arkansas NAACP, were twice turned away at the school by white mobs and the Arkansas National Guard. It was only after 11,500 soldiers were dispatched to the scene that the students were able to attend their classes in Central High.

At the same time that Little Rock activists were gearing up for their school desegregation battle, Montgomery activists were celebrating their victory over segregated city buses. The Montgomery bus boycott had lasted thirteen months, during which time the city's black residents found alternative transportation or walked. The leader of the boycott was the young pastor of the Dexter Avenue Baptist Church, **Martin Luther King Jr.** (1929–1968).

King became the nation's best-known and most respected leader in the battle for desegregation. From Montgomery to Atlanta, from Birmingham to Selma, King made the desegregation of public accommodations and voting rights his life's work. His most enduring appeal for integration, the words of which remain indelibly etched in the American consciousness, was his "I Have A Dream" speech delivered at the March on Washington for Jobs and Freedom on August 28, 1963.

Another of America's great integrationists was **John Lewis** (1940–), formerly chairman of the Student Nonviolent Coordinating Committee (SNCC; pronounced "snick"; a 1960s organization of student civil rights workers) and currently a representative to the U.S. Congress from Georgia. Lewis was a leader of the student sit-in movement in Nashville, Tennessee, in 1960. (Sit-ins were a form of civil rights protest in which black students, sometimes joined by white students, would request service at segregated lunch counters, then refuse to leave when denied service.) He also participated in the 1961 Freedom Rides (bus rides by integrated groups of people from Washington, D.C., to Jackson, Mississippi, that tested the

John Lewis speaking at a rally. In 1963 Lewis delivered one of the most powerful speeches at the March on Washington for Jobs and Freedom.
Reproduced by permission of Corbis-Bettmann.

enforcement of a Supreme Court ruling barring segregation in interstate transportation).

In 1963, Lewis delivered a powerful speech before 250,000 people at the March on Washington for Jobs and Freedom. At that time, as SNCC chairman, he was a two-year veteran of the SNCC's desegregation and voter registration work in the Deep South. There he and his fellow SNCC workers were constantly confronted with intimidation and violence by ardent segregationists. In his speech at the national march, Lewis conveyed the anger and frustration of those who were truly in the trenches of the battle for civil rights.

On July 2, 1964, President Lyndon B. Johnson (1908–1973) signed into law the 1964 Civil Rights Act (CRA), which had been proposed a year earlier by President John F. Kennedy (1917–1963). The CRA was the most expansive piece of civil rights legislation of the twentieth century. It prohibited discrimination in employment and public accommoda-

tions (such as restaurants, hotels, stores, libraries, swimming pools, parks, and theaters), and hastened the pace of school desegregation.

The CRA fell short, however, in the arena of voting rights. Throughout the South, African Americans were kept from registering to vote by literacy tests (tests selectively administered to blacks that required the applicant to read and interpret a section of the state constitution to the satisfaction of the registrar), economic intimidation (such as threats of job loss), and outright violence.

Nowhere in the South were the effects of these discriminatory measures felt as greatly as they were in Mississippi. In 1960, only 5 percent of all blacks in that state were registered to vote. For this reason, the SNCC concentrated its efforts on voter registration in Mississippi. Of all the local leaders who emerged during the SNCC's Mississippi campaign, none was more effective or determined than **Fannie Lou Hamer** (1917–1977).

Demonstrators in support of the Mississippi Freedom Democratic Party stage an all-night vigil at the Democratic Party convention in 1964.
Reproduced by permission of AP/Wide World Photos.

Hamer was a forty-four-year-old agricultural worker from rural Sunflower County, Mississippi, when she joined the SNCC's voter registration campaign in 1962. In the summer of 1964 Hamer participated in the formation of a new political party, the Mississippi Freedom Democratic Party (MFDP). The purpose of the MFDP was to serve as an alternative to the regular Democratic Party, which excluded blacks.

On August 24, 1964, an MFDP delegation traveled to Atlantic City, New Jersey, to the national Democratic Party convention. The MFDP delegates requested that they be seated in place of the regular Democrats. They claimed that the MFDP was much more representative of the people of Mississippi than was the regular Democratic Party.

The decision regarding which delegation to recognize was left to the convention's credentials committee. Several MFDP members and supporters testified before the credentials committee. The most compelling testimony—which questioned the very essence of American values—was from Fannie Lou Hamer.

Although the MFDP was not seated at the 1964 convention, the televised proceedings thrust the terrible conditions facing blacks in Mississippi and the injustice of Jim Crow laws into the national spotlight. In 1965, following a long campaign for voting rights in Selma, Alabama (during which the nation was shocked by police brutality against nonviolent demonstrations), Congress passed the Voting Rights Act (VRA). The VRA outlawed all practices used to deny blacks the right to vote and empowered federal registrars to register black voters. Immediately following the VRAs passage, the number of black voters surged throughout the South.

Kenneth B. Clark

"How Children Learn about Race"

**Excerpt from *The Eyes on the Prize Civil Rights Reader*
Published in 1991**

In 1954 the Supreme Court unanimously ruled in *Brown v. Board of Education of Topeka, Kansas* that segregated schools, while separate, were "inherently unequal." The Court wrote that "in the field of public education the doctrine of 'separate but equal' has no place." *Brown* was widely hailed as the most significant victory in the history of civil rights litigation.

Brown v. Board of Education was actually a group of five lawsuits regarding public school segregation brought by attorneys for the National Association for the Advancement of Colored People (NAACP) in five locations: Topeka, Kansas; Clarendon County, South Carolina; Prince Edward County, Virginia; Washington, D.C.; and Wilmington, Delaware. The Supreme Court chose to hear arguments for all cases on the same day, December 9, 1952. The strategy of the NAACP legal team, led by Thurgood Marshall (1908–1993), was to demonstrate that segregated schools, in a variety of states, provided lower quality education for black students than they did for white students.

Among the evidence presented by the NAACP lawyers in their cases was the research of noted black psychologist Ken-

"The racial ideas of children are less rigid, more easily changed, than the racial ideas of adults.... The direction these attitudes will take, their intensity and form of expression, will be determined by the type of experiences that the child is permitted to have."

neth B. Clark. Clark had conducted interviews with black schoolchildren using dolls of different skin colors. He found that the children preferred the white dolls and were loath to identify with the black dolls. The children's responses to Clark's questions indicated that they had low self-esteem and a poor image of their race. Clark concluded that the children had suffered psychological damage—damage could be linked to their segregated education.

"Segregation was, is, the way in which a society tells a group of human beings that they are inferior to other groups of human beings in the society," Clark stated in an interview in *Eyes on the Prize*. "It really is internalized in children, learning they cannot go to the same schools as other children, that they are required to attend clearly inferior schools than others are permitted to attend. It influences the child's view of himself."

Things to remember while reading the "How Children Learn about Race":

- The following text is the written summary of Clark's findings, presented to the Supreme Court by NAACP lawyer Thurgood Marshall during arguments in *Brown v. Board of Education of Topeka, Kansas*. Clark, with his wife Mamie Clark, had conducted his interviews with black schoolchildren in 1940. The couple's findings were first published in 1940 in the *Journal of Experimental Education*. Clark revised the language of his report in 1955, making it accessible to a general audience, and published it under the title *Prejudice and Your Child*.

- Marshall merely presented Clark's report in a written brief and did not call upon Clark to testify, because some members of the NAACP legal defense team doubted the relevance of Clark's psychological study to the legal issue at hand. To the lawyers' surprise, Supreme Court chief justice Earl Warren cited Clark's study as a key factor in the court's decision.

- In his study Clark refers to black people as "Negroes." "Negro" was a commonly accepted term at the time. In the latter half of the 1960s, "black" replaced "Negro" as the preferred word for persons of African heritage. In the 1980s and 1990s, the term "African American" came into popular use.

"How Children Learn about Race"

Are children born with racial feelings? Or do they have to learn, first, what color they are and, second, what color is "best"?

Less than fifty years ago, some social theorists maintained that racial and religious prejudices are inborn—that they are inherent and instinctive. These theorists believed that children do not have to learn to dislike people who differ from them in physical characteristics; it was considered natural to dislike those different from oneself and to like those similar to oneself.

However, research over the past thirty years has refuted these earlier theories. Social scientists are now convinced that children learn social, racial, and religious prejudices in the course of observing, and being influenced by, the existence of patterns in the culture in which they live. Students of the problem are now facing these questions:

1. How and when do children learn to identify themselves with some people and to differentiate themselves from others?

2. How and when do children acquire racial attitudes and begin to express these attitudes in their behavior?

3. What conditions in the environment foster the development of these racial attitudes and behavior?

4. What can be done to prevent the development and expression of destructive racial prejudices in children?

Until quite recently, there were differences in opinion concerning the age at which children develop and express racial prejudices. Some observers (in the tradition of those who believed that prejudices are inborn) said that even infants express racial preferences and that therefore such preferences play little or no role in the life of the child until the early teens. They pointed out that children of different races have been observed playing together and sometimes developing close friendship; this fact, they thought, showed that young children are unaware of racial or religious differences.

Within the past two decades, social scientists have made a series of studies of this problem. They indicate, on the one hand, that there is no evidence that racial prejudices are inborn; and, on the other hand, that it is equally false to assume that the child remains unaffected by racial considerations until his teens or preteens.

Racial attitudes appear early in the life of children and affect the ideas and behavior of children in the first grades of school. Such attitudes—which appear to be almost inevitable in children in our society—develop gradually.

According to one recent study, white kindergarten children in New York City show a clear preference for whites and a clear rejection of Negroes. Other studies show that Negro children in the kindergarten and early elementary grades of a New England town, in New York City, in Philadelphia, and in two urban communities in Arkansas know the difference between Negroes and whites; realize they are Negro or white; and are aware of the social meaning and evaluation of racial differences.

The development of racial awareness and racial preferences in Negro children has been studied by the author and his wife. To determine the extent of consciousness of skin color in these children between three and seven years old, we showed the children four dolls all from the same mold and dressed alike; the only difference in the dolls was that two were brown and two were white. We asked the children to choose among the dolls in answer to certain requests:

1. "Give me the white doll."

2. "Give me the colored doll."

3. "Give me the Negro doll."

These children reacted with strong awareness of skin color. Among three-year-old Negro children in both northern and southern communities, more than 75 per cent showed that they were conscious of the difference between "white" and "colored." Among older children, an increasingly greater number made the correct choices.

These findings clearly support the conclusion that racial awareness is present in Negro children as young as three years old. Furthermore, this knowledge develops in stability and clarity from year to year, and by the age of seven it is a part of the knowledge of all Negro children. Other investigators have shown that the same is true of white children.

Some children whose skin color is indistinguishable from that of white people, but who are nonetheless classified as Negroes by the society, have difficulty in making a correct racial identification of themselves at an age when other children do so. Soon, however—by the age of five or six—the majority of these children also begin to accept the social definition of themselves, even though this differs from their observance of their own skin color.

There is now no doubt that children learn the prevailing social ideas about racial differences early in their lives. Not only are they aware of race in terms of physical characteristics such as skin color, but also they are generally able to identify themselves in terms of race.

The problem of the development and awareness of religious ideas and identification in children involves more subtle and complex dis-

tinctions which understandably require a longer period of time before they are clearly understood.

It is much more difficult for children to know if they are Catholic, Protestant, or Jewish than it is to know if they are white or Negro. In one study (Radke, Trager, and Davis), children were shown pictures of a church with a cross, and of a building clearly marked as a synagogue. The investigators asked the children their reactions to these pictures. Only a minority of children between the ages of five and eight made stable and accurate identification of themselves in terms of religion. Less than half the Jewish children in this age group identified themselves as Jews, while only 30 per cent of the Catholic children and less than 27 per cent of the white Protestant children made correct religious identifications. The relatively high percentage of Jewish children who identified themselves as Jews indicates that for these children there is an earlier awareness of religious identification and probably of minority status.

In these tests, no Negro child identified himself in religious terms. This fact probably indicates that for the Negro child at these ages the dominant factor in self-identification is skin color. The impact of their minority status as determined by skin color is so great that it precludes more abstract bases for self-identification.

A study of seven- and eight-year-old Jewish boys (by Hartley, Rosenbaum, and Schwartz) found that these boys had a generalized preference for all things "Jewish." The children responded to all questions concerning self-identification and preference with such comments as: "Because I am Jewish." "Because I like Jewish." "Because they are Jewish like me." "Because I like to play with Jewish people."

This undifferentiated preference for Jewishness was found by Radke to be appreciably less among Jewish children of ten and eleven, and even less in thirteen- and fourteen-year-olds. It is possible that as these children mature their increased contact with the larger culture results in a decreased interest in Jewishness as such. It is also possible that this tendency reflects an increase in rejection of Jewishness—indicating the children's growing awareness of the minority status of Jews in America.

The same social scientists have studied small groups of Jewish, Catholic, Negro, and white Protestant children in New York City. These children were asked to respond to the simple question, "What are you?" Jewish children on all age levels answered by the term "Jewish," rarely identifying themselves in terms of nationality or color. On the other hand, a considerable proportion of the non-Jewish children identified themselves in terms of nationality rather than religion.

Non-Jewish children between the ages of 3 and 4 were usually not certain what religion they belonged to. Some non-Jewish white children in this age group said that they were Jewish; the fact that they were enrolled in a Jewish neighborhood center may have accounted for their mistaken belief that they were Jewish. At this stage of development, a non-Jewish child in a Jewish setting may conceive of himself as Jewish, and vice versa. These results suggest that the problem of religious identification involves a level of abstract thinking of which pre-school children are generally incapable.

These investigators also studied the meaning of such terms as "Jewish" and "Catholic" for children between the ages of four and ten. They found that at these ages the concepts are understood in terms of concrete activities. Jewish children mentioned "Going to shul," "Not eating bacon," or "Talking Jewish." Catholic children mentioned "Going to church," "Making communion," or "To speak as a Catholic."

Certain conclusions arise from the many independent investigations of the development of racial awareness and identification in children. By the age of four, Negro and white children are generally aware of differences in skin color and can identify themselves correctly in terms of such differences. Jewish children are not consistently aware of their Jewishness until around the age of five. The average Catholic or Protestant child does not begin to identify himself in religious terms until around seven or eight. Thus it appears that the concrete and perceptible fact of skin color provides a basis for earlier self-identification and preferences in American children than the more abstract factor of the family religion.

A child gradually learns what status the society accords to his group. The tendency of older Jewish children to show less preference for Jewishness than younger Jewish children suggests that they have learned that Jews do not have a preferred status in the larger society, and that these children have accordingly modified their self-appraisal. This effect of the awareness of the status of one's own group is even more clearly apparent in the case of Negro children.

In addition to Negro children's awareness of differences in skin color, the author and his wife studied the ability of these children to identify themselves in racial terms. We asked the children to point out the doll "which is more like you." Approximately two-thirds of all the

Kenneth B. Clark

Kenneth Bancroft Clark was born to Jamaican parents in 1914 in the Panama Canal Zone, where his father worked as a supervisor for the United Fruit Company. When Clark was four years old his mother brought him and his younger sister to New York City, where she believed they would have better educational opportunities. The family lived at the edge of Harlem, and Clark attended a mostly white elementary school. In the mid-1920s, when Clark began junior high school, the neighborhood in which he was living became predominantly black. When the few remaining whites left, Clark found himself in a segregated school.

Against the advice of his guidance counselors, who tried to shuffle all black students to vocational schools, Clark applied and was accepted to the prestigious, mostly white, George Washington High School. After graduating from high school, Clark enrolled in the predominantly black Howard University in Washington, D.C. (he selected Howard because most predominantly white colleges openly discriminated against African Americans at that time—the early 1930s).

At Howard, Clark was accepted into a circle of intellectuals and social reformers who believed in the promise of a multiracial democracy. Clark also became a writer and editor for the campus newspaper, *The Hilltop*. On one occasion Clark was arrested at the Capitol with a handful of other students, protesting a segregated restaurant inside the building.

After earning bachelor's and master's degrees from Howard in 1937, Clark entered a Ph.D. program in experimental psychology at Columbia University (he was the first African American student accepted to the graduate school). That spring he married Mamie Phipps, a student at Howard University.

children answered correctly. Correct answers were more frequent among the older ones. (Only 37 per cent of the three-year-olds but 87 per cent of the seven-year-olds responded accurately.) Negro children of light skin color had more difficulty in choosing the brown doll than Negro children of medium-brown or dark-brown skin color. This was true for older as well as younger children.

Many personal and emotional factors probably affected the ability of these Negro children to select the brown doll. In an effort to determine their racial preferences, we asked the children the following four questions:

Kenneth B. Clark. *Reproduced by permission of the estate of Raimondo Borea.*

In 1938 Phipps became involved in a study of racial identification in young children—the topic on which she wrote her master's thesis. That work became the foundation of Kenneth and Mamie Clark's later studies on the effect of segregation on the self-image of black children. In the couple's most famous study, they presented African American children with black and white dolls. Asked which doll was "good," most of the children selected the white one; many of the children cried when admitting that the black doll was the one most like themselves. This ground-breaking research was later used to support the NAACP's 1954 case for the desegregation of public schools, *Brown v. Board of Education of Topeka, Kansas.*

"I was very, very happy," stated Clark in an interview in *Eyes on the Prize,* "when Thurgood [Marshall] called me at the college on May 17, 1954, and told me not only that the decision [to eliminate segregation] had come down but that Justice Warren had specifically mentioned the psychological testimony as key."

1. *"Give me the doll that you like to play with"* or *"the doll you like best."*

2. *"Give me the doll that is the nice doll."*

3. *"Give me the doll that looks bad."*

4. *"Give me the doll that is a nice color."*

The majority of these Negro children at each age indicated an unmistakable preference for the white doll and a rejection of the brown doll.

*Studies of the development of racial awareness, racial identification, and racial preference in both Negro and white children thus present a consistent pattern. Learning about races and racial differences, learning one's own racial identity, learning which race is to be preferred and which rejected—all these are **assimilated** by the child as part of the total pattern of ideas he acquires about himself and the society in which he lives. These acquired patterns of social and racial ideas are interrelated both in development and in function. The child's first awareness of racial differences is found to be associated with some **rudimentary** evaluation of these differences. Furthermore, as the average child learns to evaluate these differences according to the standards of the society, he is at the same time required to identify himself with one or another group. This identification necessarily involves a knowledge of the status assigned to the group with which he identifies himself, in relation to the status of other groups. The child therefore cannot learn what racial group he belongs to without being involved in a larger pattern of emotions, conflict, and desires which are part of his growing knowledge of what society thinks about his race.*

Many independent studies enable us to begin to understand how children learn about race, how they identify themselves and others in terms of racial, religious, or nationality differences, and what meaning these differences have for the growing child. Racial and religious identification involves the ability of the child to identify himself with others of similar characteristics, and to distinguish himself from those who appear to be dissimilar.

The fact that young Negro children would prefer to be white reflects their knowledge that society prefers white people. White children are generally found to prefer their white skin—an indication that they too know that society likes white better. It is clear, therefore, that the self-acceptance or self-rejection found so early in a child's developing complex of racial ideas reflects the awareness and acceptance of the prevailing racial attitudes in his community.

Some children as young as three years of age begin to express racial and religious attitudes similar to those held by adults in their society. The racial and religious attitudes of sixth-graders are more definite than the attitudes of pre-school children, and hardly distinguishable from the attitudes of high-school students. Thereafter there is an increase in the intensity and complexity of these attitudes, until they become similar (at least, as far as words go) to the prevailing attitudes held by the average adult American.

Assimilated: Became absorbed into, or resembled, one's surroundings.

Rudimentary: Basic or undeveloped.

American Civil Rights: Primary Sources

The racial ideas of children are less rigid, more easily changed, than the racial ideas of adults. It is probable, too, that racial attitudes and behavior are more directly related among adults. The racial and religious attitudes of a young child may become more positive or more negative as he matures. The direction these attitudes will take, their intensity and form of expression, will be determined by the type of experiences that the child is permitted to have. One student of this problem says that, although children tend to become more tolerant in their general social attitudes as they grow older, they become less tolerant in their attitudes toward the Negro. This may reflect the fact that the things children are taught about the Negro and the experiences they are permitted to have usually result in the development of racial intolerance. (Clayborne et al, pp. 74–81)

What happened next...

Although the Supreme Court's decision in *Brown v. Board of Education of Topeka, Kansas* outlawed school segregation, it did not result in the immediate desegregation of schools. The ruling was vigorously resisted by most school officials, lawmakers at every level of government, and groups of white citizens throughout the South. The implementation of *Brown* was a slow and painful process that took as long as fifteen years in many school districts.

Many southern lawmakers referred to May 17, 1954—the date on which the *Brown* decision was rendered—as "Black Monday." One hundred and one of the 128 southern congressional representatives and senators signed the Southern Manifesto, a document denouncing the *Brown* decision and urging white southerners to "resist forced integration by any lawful means."

Brown was declared void by the legislatures of six states: Virginia, Alabama, Georgia, Mississippi, South Carolina, and Louisiana. Many states passed new, stricter school segregation laws or imposed penalties on school districts that carried out desegregation plans. Also in response to *Brown*, white southerners joined the Ku Klux Klan and other white supremacist groups in record numbers. Accordingly, there was a rise in

Members of the "Little Rock Nine" at Little Rock, Arkansas' Central High School in September 1957. On two occasions, the nine black students selected to integrate the school were physically barred from entering the premises by mobs and National Guardsmen. *Reproduced by permission of AP/Wide World Photos.*

the number of lynchings (illegal execution, by a mob, usually by hanging) and other forms of violence against blacks in the years following *Brown*.

In 1955 the Supreme Court diminished the promise of Brown by failing to set a timetable for school desegregation. The court's instructions for the enforcement of desegregation, commonly called "Brown II," stated ambiguously that desegregation must occur with "all deliberate speed." The Supreme Court advised that integration proceed at a reasonable pace and left matters of enforcement to the federal district courts. Brown II had the effect of sanctioning the foot-dragging tactics of public officials.

Many school desegregation battles took place throughout the South during the years following *Brown*. The battles typically involved mobs of hostile whites, often aided by law enforcement officials, trying to prevent black students from entering "white" schools. The most famous school desegregation confrontation occurred in Little Rock, Arkansas, in 1957.

According to a plan for gradual desegregation drafted by the Little Rock school board, a small number of black students would be admitted to Little Rock Central High School in September 1957. The nine black students selected to integrate the school were physically barred from entering the school twice, by menacing mobs and National Guardsmen. It was not until President Dwight D. Eisenhower (1890–1969) dispatched 11,500 soldiers to Little Rock to escort the nine students into the school that they were allowed to begin their educations. Armed guards ensured the students' safety for the remainder of the school year.

In 1957 the Supreme Court strengthened the force of *Brown* with its ruling in *Cooper v. Aaron.* In that case the NAACP appealed a lower court ruling that granted the Little Rock school board a two-and-a-half-year reprieve in instituting its desegregation plans. (William G. Cooper was a member of the school board, and John Aaron was one of the nine black students who had integrated Central High.)

On September 29, 1958, the Supreme Court sided with the NAACP. The justices wrote in a unanimous decision that "...the Constitutional rights of children not to be discriminated against in school admission on grounds of race or color declared by this court in the *Brown* case can neither be nullified openly and directly...nor nullified indirectly...through evasive schemes for segregation." The *Cooper* decision reaffirmed the Supreme Court's unanimous support of *Brown.*

Even after *Cooper,* many school officials continued to devise ways to avoid desegregation. An example of a drastic plan occurred in Prince Edward County, Virginia, where all public schools were closed from 1959 to 1964. During those years white students went to private schools and black students received no education at all. Some school boards delayed the desegregation with protracted court battles while others allowed only a few "token" blacks to enter selected schools (generally those in poor white neighborhoods). In some school districts boundaries were redrawn to create racially segregated schools based on residential patterns. When other tactics failed, white communities relied on the Ku Klux Klan to intimidate black parents from sending their children to "white" schools.

As a result of all these factors, by 1960—six years after the *Brown* decision—only 6.4 percent of black schoolchildren in the South attended integrated schools. There was no major progress in school desegregation until the passage of the 1964 Civil Rights Act. In addition to mandating the immediate desegregation of public schools, that legislation prohibited discrimination in employment, voting, and public accommodations (such as restaurants, hotels, stores, libraries, swimming pools, parks, and theaters). According to the legislation, segregated southern school districts were required to present desegregation plans, satisfactory to the U.S. Office of Education, in order to receive federal funding. By 1968 32 percent of black school children in the South were attending desegregated schools; by 1972 that percentage had risen to 46.

The larger implication of the *Brown* ruling was that it laid the legal groundwork for dismantling Jim Crow—the web of laws and social customs, developed in the early 1890s, that dictated the separation of the races on every level of society. The Jim Crow system had been sanctioned by the Supreme Court in 1896, in the case *Plessy v. Ferguson*. The *Plessy* decision upheld a Louisiana law mandating separate railroad cars for black and white passengers. In the *Brown* decision the court stated that the doctrine of "separate but equal" was no longer acceptable.

The Supreme Court undid the legacy of *Plessy* in a series of rulings between 1955 and 1957. The first ruling ordered the desegregation of golf courses; subsequent rulings outlawed segregated beaches, swimming pools, and public transportation. As with the case of public schools, it was many years after being declared unconstitutional that these facilities became integrated.

Did you know...

- Mamie Clark, who had recently married Kenneth Clark, pioneered the doll study while she was a student at Howard University. Kenneth Clark, most likely because he was male and held a doctorate degree, was given the lion's share of the credit for the landmark research.

- In 1945 Kenneth and Mamie Clark established the Northside Center for Child Development in Harlem—an institution that continues to operate today. In addition to serving as a mental health clinic for youths, the center has served as a policy institute. Researchers at the center have produced plans for broadening the educational opportunities available to racial minority youth, combating poverty, and encouraging urban renewal.

For More Information See

Books

Clark, Kenneth B. *Prejudice and Your Child.* Rev. 2nd ed. Middletown, CT: Wesleyan University Press, 1988.

Sources

Books

African Americans: Voices of Triumph: Perseverance. Alexandria, VA: Time-Life Books, 1993.

Altman, Susan. *Encyclopedia of African-American Heritage.* New York: Facts on File, Inc., 1997.

Clayborne, Carson, David J. Garrow, Gerald Gill, Vincent Harding, and Darlene Clark Hine, eds. *The Eyes on the Prize Reader.* New York: Penguin Books, 1991.

Kluger, Richard. *Simple Justice: The History of* Brown v. Board of Education *and Black America's Struggle for Equality.* New York: Vintage Books, 1975.

Levy, Peter B. *The Civil Rights Movement.* Westwood, CT: Greenwood Press, 1998.

Markowitz, Gerald, and David Rosner. *Children, Race, and Power: Kenneth and Mamie Clark's Northside Center.* Charlottesville, VA: University Press of Virginia, 1996.

Salmond, John A. *My Mind Set on Freedom: A History of the Civil Rights Movement, 1954–1968.* Chicago: Ivan R. Dee, 1997.

Williams, Juan. *Eyes on the Prize: America's Civil Rights Years, 1954–1965.* New York: Penguin Books, 1987.

Daisy Bates

"She Walked Alone"

Excerpt from *The Long Shadow of Little Rock: A Memoir*
Published in 1962

In 1954 the Supreme Court's ruling in *Brown v. Board of Education of Topeka, Kansas* unanimously outlawed segregation in public schools. In their decision the justices wrote that "in the field of public education the doctrine of 'separate but equal' has no place." The *Brown* decision was widely hailed as the most significant victory in the history of civil rights litigation.

Although the Brown ruling ended legal school segregation, enforcing the order was another matter. Southern school officials, lawmakers, and white citizens' groups vigorously resisted the ruling. The desegregation of schools was a long, painful process that only came about through the ceaseless efforts of civil rights activists. It was not until fifteen years after the *Brown* ruling that a significant level of integration took place throughout the South.

Brown was declared invalid by the legislatures of six states: Virginia, Alabama, Georgia, Mississippi, South Carolina, and Louisiana. Several southern states passed new, stricter school segregation laws or imposed penalties on school districts that went ahead with desegregation. The vast majority of southern congressional representatives and senators signed

"We will kneel-in, we will sit-in, until we can eat in any counter in the United States. We will walk until we are free, until we can ... take our children to any school in the United States. And we will sit-in and we will kneel-in and we will lie-in if necessary until every Negro in America can vote."

Daisy Bates at the 1963 March on Washington

Soldiers at Little Rock's Central High School. On September 2, 1957— the night before the scheduled integration of the school—Arkansas' segregationist governor Orville Faubus ordered that it be surrounded by 250 members of the Arkansas National Guard.
Reproduced by permission of AP/Wide World Photos.

the Southern Manifesto—a document denouncing the *Brown* decision and urging white southerners to "resist forced integration by any lawful means."

Many white individuals in the South responded to *Brown* by joining the Ku Klux Klan and other white supremacist groups in record numbers. In the years following *Brown*, there was a sudden rise in the number of lynchings (illegal execution, by a mob, usually by hanging) and other forms of violence against blacks.

In a 1955 decision commonly called "Brown II," the Supreme Court issued instructions for the enforcement of school desegregation. To the disappointment of African Americans, the Court failed to set a timetable. The justices stated ambiguously that desegregation must occur with "all deliberate speed" and left matters of enforcement to the federal district courts. Segregationist officials interpreted Brown II as judicial endorsement of their foot-dragging tactics.

In the years following *Brown,* struggles for school desegregation took place in many southern locations. The battle lines were typically drawn between mobs of hostile whites, often aided by law enforcement officials, and black schoolchildren trying to enter school buildings. The most famous school desegregation confrontation occurred in Little Rock, Arkansas, in 1957.

On May 22, 1954, just five days after the *Brown* decision was announced, the Little Rock school board wrote in a memo that it "is our responsibility to comply with federal constitutional requirements, and we intend to do so when the Supreme Court of the United States outlines the methods to be followed." In the fall of 1954 Little Rock school superintendent Virgil T. Blossom presented his plan—the integration of Little Rock's two high schools would come in September 1956, and the integration of the junior high schools would follow in September 1957.

Four students meet with Daisy Bates (far left) in her Little Rock, Arkansas, home. In 1957 Bates, then president of the Arkansas NAACP, helped the "Little Rock Nine" obtain a federal court order granting the students permission to enter Central High School. *Reproduced by permission of AP/Wide World Photos.*

The Blossom Plan immediately encountered resistance from segregationists. The following May the Little Rock school board presented a more modest plan, known as the "phase plan". The phase plan called for the admittance of a small number of black students to one of the high schools—Central High School—in September 1957, and gradual integration of Little Rock's junior high schools beginning in the fall of 1960.

Little Rock's segregationists were still not placated. By the end of the summer of 1957, white opposition had grown to a groundswell. On September 2, 1957, the night before the scheduled integration of Central High by nine black students, Arkansas' segregationist governor, Orville Faubus, went into action. Faubus declared in a televised news conference that it would "not be possible to restore or to maintain order...if forcible integration is carried out tomorrow." After claiming that "blood will run in the streets if Negro pupils should attempt to enter Central High School," Faubus ordered the school to be surrounded by 250 members of the Arkansas National Guard. Although Faubus's stated objective for this action was to keep the peace, it soon became clear that the guardsmen's purpose was to prevent the black students from entering the school.

The nine black students (known as the "Little Rock Nine") did not to try to enter the school on September 3. Instead, with the assistance of Daisy Bates, president of the Arkansas National Association for the Advancement of Colored People (NAACP), and NAACP lawyers, the students obtained a federal court order granting them admission to the school. The next morning, September 4, the Little Rock Nine made their first attempt to enter Central High.

Things to remember while reading "She Walked Alone":

- Student Elizabeth Eckford approached the school alone because she did not know about the other students' plans to meet. Daisy Bates had notified the other eight students by phone to meet at an appointed place, where they were to pile into two police cars for the ride to school. The Eckford family had no phone, and Bates failed to get the message to Elizabeth.

- The hostility of the segregationist crowd in Little Rock was an all too common phenomenon in the South. Since the 1890s the South had been ruled by Jim Crow laws—the set of legislation and social customs that dictated the separation of the races on every level of society. White supremacist groups and segregationist mobs had an extensive history of acting, in intimidating and violent ways, to preserve the Jim Crow system. That such hostility was exhibited in Little Rock, however, was surprising. Little Rock was considered a politically moderate community with relatively good race relations.

"She Walked Alone"

What follows is a description of the events that confronted Elizabeth Eckford, the only student of the Little Rock Nine to approach Central High alone, on the morning of September 4.

Dr. Benjamin Fine was then education editor of the New York Times. *He had years before won for his newspaper a Pulitzer prize. He was among the first reporters on the scene to cover the Little Rock story.*

A few days after the National Guard blocked the Negro children's entrance to the school, Ben showed up at my house. He paced the floor nervously, rubbing his hands together as he talked.

"Daisy, they spat in my face. They called me a 'dirty Jew.' I've been a marked man ever since the day Elizabeth tried to enter Central. I never told you what happened that day. I tried not to think about it. Maybe I was ashamed to admit to you or to myself that white men and women could be so beastly cruel.

"I was standing in front of the school that day. Suddenly there was a shout—'They're here! The niggers are coming!' I saw a sweet little girl who looked about fifteen, walking alone. She tried several times to pass through the guards. The last time she tried, they put their bayonets in front of her. When they did this, she became panicky. For a moment she just stood there trembling. Then she seemed to calm down and started walking toward the bus stop with the mob baying at her heels like a pack of hounds. The women were shouting,

'Get her! **Lynch** her!' The men were yelling, 'Go home, you bastard of a black bitch!' She finally made it to the bus stop and sat down on the bench. I sat down beside her and said, 'I'm a reporter from The New York Times, may I have your name?' She just sat there, her head down. Tears were streaming down her cheeks from under her sunglasses. Daisy, I don't know what made me put my arm around her, lifting her chin, saying, 'Don't let them see you cry.' Maybe she reminded me of my fifteen-year-old daughter, Jill.

"There must have been five hundred around us by this time. I vaguely remember someone hollering, 'Get a rope and drag her over to this tree.' Suddenly I saw a white-haired, kind-faced woman fighting her way through the mob. She looked at Elizabeth, and then screamed at the mob, 'Leave this child alone! Why are you tormenting her? Six months from now, you will hang your heads in shame.' The mob shouted, 'Another nigger-lover. Get out of here!' The woman, who I found out later was Mrs. Grace Lorch, the wife of Dr. Lee Lorch, professor at Philander Smith College, turned to me and said, 'We have to do something. Let's try to get a cab.'

"We took Elizabeth across the street to the drugstore. I remained on the sidewalk with Elizabeth while Mrs. Lorch tried to enter the drugstore to call a cab. But the hoodlums slammed the door in her face and wouldn't let her in. She pleaded with them to call a cab for the child. They closed in on her saying, 'Get out of here, you bitch!' Just then the city bus came. Mrs. Lorch and Elizabeth got on. Elizabeth must have been in a state of shock. She never uttered a word. When the bus pulled away, the mob closed in around me. 'We saw you put your arm around that little bitch. Now it's your turn.' A drab, middle-aged woman said viciously, 'Grab him and kick him in the balls!' A girl I had seen hustling in one of the local bars screamed, 'A dirty New York Jew! Get him!' A man asked me, 'Are you a Jew?' I said, 'Yes.' He then said to the mob, 'Let him be! We'll take care of him later.'

"The irony of it all, Daisy, is that during all this time the national guardsmen made no effort to protect Elizabeth or to help me. Instead, they threatened to have me arrested—for inciting to riot."

Elizabeth, whose dignity and control in the face of jeering mobsters had been filmed by television cameras and recorded in pictures flashed to newspapers over the world, had overnight become a national heroine. During the next few days newspaper reporters besieged her home, wanting to talk to her. The first day that her parents agreed she might come out of seclusion, she came to my house where the reporters awaited her. Elizabeth was very quiet, speaking

Lynch: Illegal execution by a mob, usually by hanging.

only when spoken to. I took her to my bedroom to talk before I let the reporters see her. I asked how she felt now. Suddenly all her pent-up emotion flared.

"Why am I here?" she said, turning blazing eyes on me. "Why are you so interested in my welfare now? You didn't care enough to notify me of the change of plans—"

I walked over and reached out to her. Before she turned her back on me, I saw tears gathering in her eyes. My heart was breaking for this young girl who stood there trying to stifle her sobs. How could I explain that frantic early morning when at three o'clock my mind had gone on strike?

In the ensuing weeks Elizabeth took part in all the activities of the nine—press conferences, attendance at court, studying with professors at nearby Philander Smith College. She was present, that is, but never really a part of things. The hurt had been too deep.

On the two nights she stayed at my home I was awakened by the screams in her sleep, as she relived in her dreams the terrifying mob

Elizabeth Eckford (far right, in sunglasses) walks to Little Rock Central High alone. Due to a miscommunication, Eckford did not know about the other "Little Rock Nine" members' plan to meet and travel to school in two police cars.
Reproduced by permission of AP/Wide World Photos.

scenes at Central. The only times Elizabeth showed real excitement were when Thurgood Marshall met the children and explained the meaning of what had happened in court. As he talked, she would listen **raptly,** a faint smile on her face. It was obvious he was her hero.

Little by little Elizabeth came out of her shell. Up to now she had never talked about what happened to her at Central. Once when we were alone in the downstairs recreation room of my house, I asked her simply, "Elizabeth, do you think you can talk about it now?"

She remained quiet for a long time. Then she began to speak.

"You remember the day before we were to go in, we met Superintendent Blossom at the school board office. He told us what the mob might say and do but he never told us we wouldn't have any protection. He told our parents not to come because he wouldn't be able to protect the children if they did.

"That night I was so excited I couldn't sleep. The next morning I was about the first one up. While I was pressing my black and white dress—I had made it to wear on the first day of school—my little brother turned on the TV set. They started telling about a large crowd gathered at the school. The man on TV said he wondered if we were going to show up that morning. Mother called from the kitchen, where she was fixing breakfast, 'Turn that TV off!' She was so upset and worried. I wanted to comfort her, so I said, 'Mother, don't worry.'

"Dad was walking back and forth, from room to room, with a sad expression. He was chewing on his pipe and he had a cigar in his hand, but he didn't light either one. It would have been funny, only he was so nervous.

"Before I left home Mother called us into the living-room. She said we should have a word of prayer. Then I caught the bus and got off a block from the school. I saw a large crowd of people standing across the street from the soldiers guarding Central. As I walked on, the crowd suddenly got very quiet. Superintendent Blossom had told us to enter by the front door. I looked at all the people and thought, 'Maybe I will be safer if I walk down the block to the front entrance behind the guards.'

"At the corner I tried to pass through the long line of guards around the school so as to enter the grounds behind them. One of the guards pointed across the street. So I pointed in the same direction and asked whether he meant for me to cross the street and walk down. He nodded 'yes.' So, I walked across the street conscious of the

American Civil Rights: Primary Sources

crowd that stood there, but they moved away from me.

"For a moment all I could hear was the shuffling of their feet. Then someone shouted, 'Here she comes, get ready!' I moved away from the crowd on the sidewalk and into the street. If the mob came at me I could then cross back over so the guards could protect me.

"The crowd moved in closer and began to follow me, calling me names. I still wasn't afraid. Just a little bit nervous. Then my knees started to shake all of a sudden and I wondered whether I could make it to the center entrance a block away. It was the longest block I ever walked in my whole life.

"Even so, I still wasn't too scared because all the time I kept thinking that the guards would protect me.

"When I got right in front of the school, I went up to a guard again. But this time he just looked straight ahead and didn't move to let me pass. I didn't know what to do. Then I looked and saw that the path leading to the front entrance was a little further ahead. So I walked until I was right in front of the path to the front door.

"I stood looking at the school—it looked so big! Just then the guards let some white students go through.

"The crowd was quiet. I guess they were waiting to see what was going to happen. When I was able to steady my knees, I walked up to the guard who had let the white students in. He too didn't move. When I tried to squeeze past him, he raised his bayonet and then the other guards closed in and they raised their bayonets.

"They glared at me with a mean look and I was very frightened and didn't know what to do. I turned around and the crowd came toward me.

"They moved closer and closer. Somebody started yelling, 'Lynch her! Lynch her!'

"I tried to see a friendly face somewhere in the mob—someone who maybe would help. I looked into the face of an old woman and it seemed a kind face, but when I looked at her again, she spat on me.

"They came closer, shouting, 'No nigger bitch is going to get in our school. Get out of here!'

"I turned back to the guards but their faces told me I wouldn't get help from them. Then I looked down the block and saw a bench at the bus stop. I thought, 'If I can only get there I will be safe.' I don't know why the bench seemed a safe place to me, but I started walking

Daisy Bates

Daisy Bates was born in 1920 in the small town of Huttig, in southeast Arkansas. When Bates was an infant, her mother was killed by three white men. Her father, unable to control his grief and anger, handed the baby over to friends to raise and left the state.

Bates attended a segregated public school in Huttig, where the students used textbooks that had been discarded by white students. At age fifteen she met Lucius Christopher (L.C.) Bates, and six years later the two wed. The couple moved to Little Rock, where they began a small, weekly paper called the *State Press*. In the pages of the paper the couple championed the rights of African Americans and exposed cases of police brutality.

In 1952 Daisy Bates became president of the Arkansas NAACP. She watched with great anticipation as the school desegregation case *Brown v. Board of Education of Topeka, Kansas* wound its way through the courts and celebrated the Supreme Court's 1954 ruling that ended segregated schools. Soon Bates found herself at the center of the Little Rock struggle over the integration of the city's Central High School. Bates served as advocate and protector of the nine black

toward it. I tried to close my mind to what they were shouting, and kept saying to myself, 'If I can only make it to the bench I will be safe.'

"When I finally got there, I don't think I could have gone another step. I sat down and the mob crowded up and began shouting all over again. Someone hollered, 'Drag her over to this tree! Let's take care of the nigger.' Just then a white man sat down beside me, put his arm around me and patted my shoulder. He raised my chin and said, 'Don't let them see you cry.'

"Then, a white lady—she was very nice—she came over to me on the bench. She spoke to me but I don't remember now what she said. She put me on the bus and sat next to me. She asked me my name and tried to talk to me but I don't think I answered. I can't remember much about the bus ride, but the next thing I remember I was standing in front of the School for the Blind, where Mother works.

"I thought, 'Maybe she isn't here. But she has to be here!' So I ran upstairs, and I think some teachers tried to talk to me, but I kept running until I reached Mother's classroom.

Daisy Bates. *Reproduced by permission of AP/Wide World Photos.*

students selected to attend the all-white high school in the fall of 1957.

White supremacists, attempting to intimidate Bates, burned two crosses on Bates's lawn and twice hurled firebombs at her home. On one occasion Bates was sprayed with shattered glass when a rock was thrown through her front window. A message tied to the rock said, "Stone this time. Dynamite next."

After the Little Rock schools had been successfully integrated, Bates turned her energies to voter registration and voter education. She continues to play an active role in several community organizations.

"Mother was standing at the window with her head bowed, but she must have sensed I was there because she turned around. She looked as if she had been crying, and I wanted to tell her I was all right. But I couldn't speak. She put her arms around me and I cried." (Bates, pp. 69–76)

What happened next...

On September 22, on orders from President Dwight D. Eisenhower (1890–1969), Governor Faubus removed the National Guard from the school. The Little Rock Nine were told to report for classes the following day.

On September 23 the Little Rock Nine once again approached Central High. There they were met by more than

1,000 white segregationists, shouting "Two, four, six, eight, we ain't gonna integrate." Somehow, the Little Rock Nine, again escorted by Daisy Bates, slipped into the school through a side door.

Once the crowd discovered that the black students were inside the school, it went wild. When it looked as though the mob was going to overtake the police barricades, the city's mayor arranged for the black students to be driven away from the building, through a delivery entrance, in two waiting cars. Soon thereafter people in the mob vandalized the school and brutally beat two black reporters.

On September 24 President Eisenhower authorized the dispatch of 11,500 soldiers, including 1,000 paratroopers from the 101st Airborne Division, to Little Rock. The next day the soldiers escorted the students to school, holding back the mob at gunpoint. For the remainder of the week each of the Little Rock Nine was accompanied to classes by an armed guard. On September 31 Eisenhower withdrew the troops. For the rest of the school year the black students were protected by federalized (brought under the jurisdiction of the federal government) Arkansas National Guardsmen.

Even after the Little Rock Nine had made it into the school, their problems were far from over. The students were subjected to daily threats and taunts throughout their years at Central High. According to Vice Principal Elizabeth Huckaby, the students were forced to endure "name-calling, thrown objects, trippings, shovings, kickings." Several of the students received phone calls threatening that they would be shot with acid-filled squirt guns.

During the 1957–1958 school year, the Little Rock school board had requested, and received, from a federal judge a two-and-a-half-year reprieve in instituting its desegregation plans. Lawyers for the NAACP appealed the case, entitled *Cooper v. Aaron,* to the Supreme Court. (The case is named for William G. Cooper, who was a member of the school board, and John Aaron, who was one of the Little Rock Nine.)

On September 29, 1958, the Supreme Court decided in favor of the NAACP. The justices wrote in a unanimous decision that "...the Constitutional rights of children not to be discriminated against in school admission on grounds of race or color declared by this court in the *Brown* case can neither be nullified openly and directly . . . nor nullified indirectly . . .through evasive schemes for segregation." The *Cooper* decision reaffirmed the Supreme Court's unanimous support of *Brown*.

Rather than comply with the Supreme Court's ruling, Governor Faubus ordered all Little Rock schools closed. He then helped white segregationists establish the all-white Little Rock Private School Corporation, to which public school buildings were leased. Nearly half of the white students of Little Rock attended the "private" schools. Many students—both black and white—received no education that year. The following September Little Rock public schools were reopened on an integrated basis.

"Events in history occur when the time has ripened for them, but they need a spark," wrote Bates in her autobiography. "Little Rock was the spark at that stage of the struggle of the American Negro for justice." The majority of southern school districts continued to resist integration even after Little Rock had acquiesced. By 1960 only 6.4 percent of black schoolchildren in the South attended integrated schools. Major progress in school desegregation had to wait until the passage of the 1964 Civil Rights Act. That landmark legislation, in addition to mandating the immediate desegregation of public schools, prohibited discrimination in employment, voting, and public accommodations (such as restaurants, hotels, stores, libraries, swimming pools, parks, and theaters). By 1968 32 percent of black schoolchildren in the South were attending desegregated schools; by 1972 that percentage had risen to 46.

Did you know...

- All but one of the Little Rock Nine graduated from Central High. The one who did not graduate, Minniejean Brown, was expelled for exchanging insults with a white student. The white student had called Brown a "nigger bitch"; Brown had responded by calling the white student "white trash." Prior to that incident, Brown had dumped chili on the head of a white boy who had been harassing her. After her expulsion from Central High, Brown moved to New York City to continue her education.

- Daisy Bates was among the speakers at the March on Washington for Jobs and Freedom. The August 28, 1963, march was attended by more than 250,000 people. "We will kneel-in, we will sit-in, until we can eat in any counter in the United States," stated Bates at the march. "We will walk until we are free, until we can ... take our children to any school in the United States. And we will sit-in and we will kneel-in and we will lie-in if necessary until every Negro in America can vote."

Sources

Books

African American Biography. Vol. 3. Detroit: U•X•L, 1994, pp. 50–53.

African Americans: Voices of Triumph: Perseverance. Alexandria, VA: Time-Life Books, 1993.

Altman, Susan. *Encyclopedia of African-American Heritage.* New York: Facts on File, Inc., 1997.

Bates, Daisy. *The Long Shadow of Little Rock: A Memoir.* New York: David McKay Company, Inc., 1962.

Kluger, Richard. *Simple Justice: The History of* Brown v. Board of Education *and Black America's Struggle for Equality.* New York: Vintage Books, 1975.

Levy, Peter B. *The Civil Rights Movement.* Westwood, CT: Greenwood Press, 1998.

Williams, Juan. *Eyes on the Prize: America's Civil Rights Years, 1954–1965.* New York: Penguin Books, 1987.

Other

Eyes on the Prize: America's Civil Rights Years (videocassette; six episodes). Boston: Blackside, Inc., 1986.

Martin Luther King Jr.

"Letter from Birmingham City Jail"
and "I Have a Dream"

Speeches reprinted in *A Testament of Hope:*
The Essential Writings of Martin Luther King Jr.
Published in 1986

During the decade known as the civil rights era, roughly from 1955 to 1965, hundreds of thousands of people demonstrated to secure the civil rights of African Americans. At stake was the right to vote, the right to attend integrated schools, and the freedom to obtain housing in any neighborhood and employment in any profession. Civil rights activists worked for an end to the Jim Crow system (the set of legislation and social customs that dictated the separation of the races at every level of society). There is no one person more closely associated with the struggle for civil rights than Martin Luther King Jr.

King was twenty-six years old and the new pastor of Montgomery, Alabama's Dexter Avenue Baptist Church when he entered the civil rights movement. In his capacity as president of the Montgomery Improvement Association (MIA), King led the 382-day-long bus boycott in 1955 and 1956 that resulted in the integration of Montgomery's bus system. King quickly rose to national prominence as the civil rights movement's most charismatic speaker and most effective leader.

> "For years now I have heard the words 'Wait!' It rings in the ear of every Negro with a piercing familiarity. This 'Wait' has almost always meant 'Never.'"

Martin Luther King Jr. speaking at the 1963 March on Washington for Jobs and Freedom.
Reproduced by permission of AP/Wide World Photos.

King served as president of the Southern Christian Leadership Conference (SCLC)—a civil rights organization comprised of southern clergymen—from its founding in 1957 until his death in 1968. In that capacity, King led campaigns for desegregation (the elimination of laws and social customs that call for the separation of races) and voting rights all throughout the South. Through his speeches and writings, which have been preserved in numerous recordings and publications, one can gain a general understanding of what transpired during the civil rights movement.

King wrote the following two documents in 1963, during the Birmingham civil rights campaign and the March on Washington for Jobs and Freedom, respectively. The purpose of the Birmingham campaign, which began in April 1963, was to desegregate the downtown area of what, in King's words, was "probably the most thoroughly segregated city in the United States."

After five weeks of boycotts of selected downtown department stores, marches, and demonstrations, an accord was reached between activists and city officials that promised an end to the segregation of downtown stores and the hiring of blacks in clerical and sales positions. That victory, however, did not come without a heavy price. Thousands of Birmingham's African American residents—young and old alike—endured beatings, jailings, attacks by police dogs, and blasts from fire hoses.

In June 1963, in response to that summer's numerous civil rights demonstrations and displays of brutality against the demonstrators, President John F. Kennedy (1917–1963) proposed a sweeping civil rights bill. That bill, which was signed into law one year later by President Lyndon B. Johnson (1908–1973) as the 1964 Civil Rights Act, promised an end to segregation of all public accommodations and a shorter timetable for school desegregation.

To demonstrate popular support for the proposed legislation, King and other civil rights leaders called for a march in the nation's capital. Two hundred fifty thousand people from all races and all walks of life converged in Washington on August 28, 1963. As the people marched, there was a feeling of optimism in the air. Reverend Ralph Abernathy (1926–1990) of the SCLC described it as "a jubilation." The march route ended at the Lincoln Memorial, where folksingers performed and civil rights leaders delivered speeches.

Things to remember while reading "Letter from Birmingham City Jail" and "I Have Dream":

- King wrote his **"Letter from Birmingham City Jail"** on April 16, 1963. He had been arrested four days earlier while leading a march to the Birmingham city hall, in defiance of a court order banning such marches. King was released on bond on April 20.

- King wrote his open letter in response to a full-page advertisement in the local paper, in which a group of eight prominent white religious leaders called the civil rights demonstrations "unwise and untimely." The clergymen stated: "We do not believe that these days of new hope are days when extreme measures [are necessary] in Birmingham." (The "new hope" referred to a newly elected mayor and city council.)

- King wrote that the SCLC had postponed its demonstrations until after the city elections had taken place that March, and that the civil rights activists wished to see Mr. Connor defeated. Eugene "Bull" Connor, Birmingham's notoriously racist and violent police commissioner, was engaged in a run-off election for mayor against moderate segregationist Albert Boutwell. So as not to influence the election in favor of Connor, the SCLC waited until Boutwell had won the race before beginning its Birmingham campaign.

- King spent his eight days in jail in solitary confinement. He had only a metal cot frame, with no mattress, to sleep on.

- King wrote his letter, which was 6,500 words in its original form, on the margins of newspaper and on sheets of toilet paper. He then had it smuggled out of jail. The letter was originally circulated as a pamphlet by the American Friends Service Committee.

- In his letter, King refers to black people as "Negroes." "Negro" was a commonly accepted term at the time. In the latter half of the 1960s, "black" replaced "Negro" as the preferred word for persons of African heritage. In the 1980s and 1990s, the term "African American" came into popular use.

- King delivered his **"I Have a Dream"** speech at the conclusion of the August 28, 1963, March for Jobs and Freedom in Washington, D.C. Before his speech, the audience had listened to folk and gospel singers including Marian Anderson, Mahalia Jackson, Odetta, Joan Baez, Bob Dylan, and Peter, Paul and Mary, and civil rights leaders such as A. Philip Randolph, Daisy Bates, Roy Wilkins, Whitney Young, and John Lewis.

- King's speech elicited the greatest response from the crowd of any of the speeches delivered at the Lincoln Memorial. On that day, King became the undisputed leader of the civil rights movement in America. The speech has become a classic of American literature.

- King's message was purposely conciliatory at a time when many African Americans were feeling resentful toward all whites, and especially the white power establishment (which was continually impeding blacks' social progress). In his speech, King stressed hopes for harmonious relations between the races.

- King's speech may have been but a footnote in history if he had delivered his remarks as originally prepared. As his speech drew to a close, Mahalia Jackson, the noted gospel singer who was seated behind King on the stage, called out "Tell them about the *dream,* Martin." She had heard King speak of his "dream" at a gathering earlier that summer and had found it moving and inspirational.

- When King spoke of the "sweltering summer of the Negro's legitimate discontent," he was referring to the explosion of civil rights activity during the spring and summer of 1963.

All told, there were some 930 demonstrations in 115 cities in eleven southern states. More than 20,000 protesters were arrested in total during those actions.

"Letter From Birmingham City Jail"

My dear Fellow Clergymen,

While confined here in the Birmingham city jail, I came across your recent statement calling our present activities "unwise and untimely." Seldom, if ever, do I pause to answer criticism of my work and ideas. If I sought to answer all of the criticisms that cross my desk, my secretaries would be engaged in little else in the course of the day, and I would have no time for constructive work. But since I feel that you are men of genuine good will and your criticisms are sincerely set forth, I would like to answer your statement in what I hope will be patient and reasonable terms.

I think I should give the reason for my being in Birmingham, since you have been influenced by the argument of "outsiders coming in." I have the honor of serving as president of the Southern Christian Leadership Conference, an organization operating in every southern state, with headquarters in Atlanta, Georgia. We have some eighty-five affiliate organizations all across the South—one being the Alabama Christian Movement for Human Rights. Whenever necessary and possible we share staff, educational and financial resources with our affiliates. Several months ago our local affiliate here in Birmingham invited us to be on call to engage in a nonviolent direct-action program if such were deemed necessary. We readily consented and when the hour came we lived up to our promises. So I am here, along with several members of my staff, because we were invited here. I am here because I have basic organizational ties here.

*Beyond this, I am in Birmingham because injustice is here. Just as the eighth century prophets left their little villages and carried their "thus saith the Lord" far beyond the boundaries of their hometowns; and just as the **Apostle Paul** left his little village of Tarsus and carried the gospel of Jesus Christ to practically every hamlet and city of the **Graeco-Roman world**, I too am compelled to carry the gospel of free-*

Apostle Paul: One of the twelve missionaries sent by Christ to preach the gospel. Paul was born in Tarsus, a village in southern Turkey.

Graeco-Roman world: In the first four centuries A.D., a region that included most of Europe, the Middle East, and Northern Africa.

dom beyond my particular hometown. Like Paul, I must constantly respond to the Macedonian call for aid.

Moreover, I am cognizant of the interrelatedness of all communities and states. I cannot sit idly by in Atlanta and not be concerned about what happens in Birmingham. Injustice anywhere is a threat to justice everywhere. We are caught in an inescapable network of mutuality, tied in a single garment of destiny. Whatever affects one directly affects all indirectly. Never again can we afford to live with the narrow, provincial "outside agitator" idea. Anyone who lives in the United States can never be considered an outsider anywhere in this country.

You deplore the demonstrations that are presently taking place in Birmingham. But I am sorry that your statement did not express a similar concern for the conditions that brought the demonstrations into being. I am sure that each of you would want to go beyond the superficial social analyst who looks merely at effects, and does not grapple with underlying causes. I would not hesitate to say that it is unfortunate that so-called demonstrations are taking place in Birmingham at this time, but I would say in more emphatic terms that it is even more unfortunate that the white power structure of this city left the Negro community with no other alternative.

In any nonviolent campaign there are four basic steps: (1) collection of the facts to determine whether injustices are alive, (2) negotiation, (3) self-purification, and (4) direct action. We have gone through all of these steps in Birmingham. There can be no gainsaying of the fact that racial injustice engulfs this community.

Birmingham is probably the most thoroughly segregated city in the United Sates. Its ugly record of police brutality is known in every section of this country. Its injust treatment of Negroes in the courts is a notorious reality. There have been more unsolved bombings of Negro homes and churches in Birmingham than any city in this nation. There are the hard, brutal and unbelievable facts. On the basis of these conditions Negro leaders sought to negotiate with the city fathers. But the political leaders consistently refused to engage in good faith negotiation.

Then came the opportunity last September to talk with some of the leaders of the economic community. In these negotiating sessions certain promises were made by the merchants—such as the promise to remove the humiliating racial signs from the stores. On the basis of these promises Rev. Shuttlesworth and the leaders of the Alabama

Macedonia: An ancient country in southern Europe, north of Greece, the inhabitants of which were enslaved by the Romans.

Mutuality: Condition of mutual dependence or reciprocity.

Provincial: Unsophisticated or narrow-minded.

Agitator: A person who rallies others to support a cause.

Gainsaying: Denying or contradicting.

Segregation: The separation of the races, as dictated by laws and social customs.

Christian Movement for Human Rights agreed to call a moratorium on any type of demonstrations. As the weeks and months unfolded we realized that we were the victims of a broken promise. The signs remained. Like so many experiences of the past we were confronted with blasted hopes, and the dark shadow of a deep disappointment settled upon us. So we had no alternative except that of preparing for direct action, whereby we would present our very bodies as a means of laying our case before the conscience of the local and national community. We were not unmindful of the difficulties involved. So we decided to go through a process of self-purification. We started having workshops on nonviolence and repeatedly asked ourselves the questions, "Are you able to accept blows without retaliating?" "Are you able to endure the ordeals of jail?" We decided to set our direct-action program around the Easter season, realizing that with the exception of Christmas, this was the largest shopping period of the year. Knowing that a strong economic withdrawal program would be the by-product of direct action, we felt that this was the best time to bring pressure on the merchants for the needed changes. Then it occurred to us that the March election was ahead and so we speedily decided to postpone action until after election day. When we discovered that Mr. Connor was in the run-off, we decided again to postpone action so that the demonstrations could not be used to cloud the issues. At this time we agreed to begin our nonviolent witness the day after the run-off.

This reveals that we did not move irresponsibly into direct action. We too wanted to see Mr. Connor defeated; so we went through postponement after postponement to aid in this community need. After this we felt that direct action could be delayed no longer.

*You may well ask, "Why direct action? Why sit-ins, marches, etc.? Isn't negotiation a better path?" You are exactly right in your call for negotiation. Indeed, this is the purpose of direct action. Nonviolent direct action seeks to create such a crisis and establish such creative tension that a community that has constantly refused to negotiate is forced to confront the issue. It seeks so to dramatize the issue that it can no longer be ignored. I just referred to the creation of tension as a part of the work of the nonviolent resister. This may sound rather shocking. But I must confess that I am not afraid of the word tension. I have earnestly worked and preached against violent tension, but there is a type of constructive nonviolent tension that is necessary for growth. Just as **Socrates** felt that it was necessary to create a tension in the mind so that individuals could rise from the bondage of myths*

Socrates: 469? B.C.– 399 B.C.; philosopher from Athens, Greece.

and half-truths to the unfettered realm of creative analysis and objective appraisal, we must see the need of having nonviolent **gadflies** to create the kind of tension in society that will help men to rise from the dark depths of prejudice and racism to the majestic heights of understanding and brotherhood. So the purpose of the direct action is to create a situation so crisis-packed that it will inevitably open the door to negotiation. We, therefore, concur with you in your call for negotiation. Too long has our beloved Southland been bogged down in the tragic attempt to live in monologue rather than dialogue.

One of the basic points in your statement is that our acts are untimely. Some have asked, "Why didn't you give the new administration time to act?" The only answer that I can give to this inquiry is that the new administration must be prodded about as much as the outgoing one before it acts. We will be sadly mistaken if we feel that the election of Mr. Boutwell will bring the **millennium** to Birmingham. While Mr. Boutwell is much more articulate and gentle than Mr. Connor, they are both **segregationists**, dedicated to the task of maintaining the status quo. The hope I see in Mr. Boutwell is that he will be reasonable enough to see the futility of massive resistance to **desegregation.** But he will not see this without pressure from the devotees of civil rights. My friends, I must say to you that we have not made a single gain in civil rights without determined legal and nonviolent pressure. History is the long and tragic story of the fact that privileged groups seldom give up their privileges voluntarily. Individuals may see the moral light and voluntarily give up their unjust posture; but as **Reinhold Niebuhr** has reminded us, groups are more immoral than individuals.

We know through painful experience that freedom is never voluntarily given by the oppressor; it must be demanded by the oppressed. Frankly, I have never yet engaged in a direct action movement that was "well-timed," according to the timetable of those who have not suffered unduly from the disease of segregation. For years now I have heard the words "Wait!" It rings in the ear of every Negro with a piercing familiarity. This "Wait" has almost always meant "Never." It has been a tranquilizing **thalidomide,** relieving the emotional stress for a moment, only to give birth to an ill-formed infant of frustration. We must come to see with the distinguished jurist of yesterday that "justice too long delayed is justice denied." We have waited for more than 340 years for our constitutional and God-given rights. The nations of Asia and Africa are moving with jetlike speed toward the goal of political independence, and we still creep at horse

Gadfly: A person who persistently promotes certain ideas, to the annoyance of others.

Millennium: A period of 1,000 years. In religious texts the term refers to the period in which Christ will reign on Earth.

Segregationist: One who promotes or enforces the separation of the races.

Desegregation: The elimination of laws and social customs that dictate the separation of the races.

Reinhold Niebuhr: 1892–1971; professor of philisophy and religion at the Union Theological Seminary in New York beginning in the 1930s. Niebuhr promoted the ideals of nonviolent revolution and was one of King's earliest and most prominent influences.

Thalidomide: Anti-nausea drug widely prescribed to women in the 1950s that was later found to cause birth defects.

and buggy pace toward the gaining of a cup of coffee at a lunch counter. I guess it is easy for those who have never felt the stinging darts of segregation to say, "Wait." But when you have seen vicious mobs lynch your mothers and fathers at will and drown your sisters and brothers at whim; when you have seen hate-filled policemen curse, kick, brutalize and even kill your black brothers and sisters with impunity; when you see the vast majority of your twenty million Negro brothers smothering in an airtight cage of poverty in the midst of an affluent society; when you suddenly find your tongue twisted and your speech stammering as you seek to explain to your six-year-old daughter why she can't go to the public amusement park that has just been advertised on television, and see tears welling up in her little eyes when she is told that Funtown is closed to colored children, and see the depressing clouds of inferiority begin to form in her little mental sky, and see her begin to distort her little personality by unconsciously developing a bitterness toward white people; when you have to concoct an answer for a five-year-old son asking in agonizing pathos: "Daddy, why do white people treat colored people so mean?"; when you take a cross-country drive and find it necessary to sleep night after night in the uncomfortable corners of your automobile because no motel will accept you; when you are humiliated day in and day out by nagging signs reading "white" and "colored"; when your first name becomes "nigger" and your middle name becomes "boy" (however old you are) and your last name becomes "John," and when your wife and mother are never given the respected title "Mrs."; when you are harried by day and haunted by night by the fact that you are a Negro, living constantly at tiptoe stance never quite knowing what to expect next, and plagued with inner fears and outer resentments; when you are forever fighting a degenerating sense of "nobodiness"; then you will understand why we find it difficult to wait. There comes a time when the cup of endurance runs over, and men are no longer willing to be plunged into an abyss of injustice where they experience the blackness of corroding despair. I hope, sirs, you can understand our legitimate and unavoidable impatience....

Oppressed people cannot remain oppressed forever. The urge for freedom will eventually come. This is what happened to the American Negro. Something within has reminded him of his birthright of freedom; something without has reminded him that he can gain it. Consciously and unconsciously, he has been swept in by what the Germans call the Zeitgeist, and with his black brothers of Africa, and his brown and yellow brothers of Asia, South America and the Caribbean, he is moving with a sense of cosmic urgency toward the promised land of racial justice. Recognizing this vital urge that has engulfed the Negro community, one should readily understand public demonstrations. The Negro has many pent-up resentments and latent frustrations. He has to get them out. So let him march sometime; let him have his prayer pilgrimages to the city hall; understand why he must have sit-ins and freedom rides. If his repressed emotions do not come out in these nonviolent ways, they will come out in ominous expression of violence. This is not a threat; it is a fact of history. So I have not said to my people "get rid of your discontent." But I have tried to say that this normal and healthy discontent can be channelized through the creative outlet of nonviolent direct action. Now this approach is being dismissed as extremist. I must admit that I was initially disappointed in being so categorized....

Let me rush on to mention my other disappointments. I have been so greatly disappointed with the white church and its leadership. Of course, there are some notable exceptions. I am not unmindful of the fact that each of you has taken some significant stands on this issue. I commend you, Rev. Stallings, for your Christian stance on this past Sunday, in welcoming Negroes to your worship service on a non-segregated basis. I commend the Catholic leaders of this state for integrating Springhill College several years ago.

But despite these notable exceptions I must honestly reiterate that I have disappointed with the church. I do not say that as one of the negative critics who can always find something wrong with the church. I say it as a minister of the gospel, who loves the church; who was nurtured in its bosom; who has been sustained by its spiritual blessings and who will remain true to it as long as the cord of life shall lengthen.

I had the strange feeling when I was suddenly catapulted into the leadership of the bus protest in Montgomery several years ago that we would have the support of the white church. I felt that the white ministers, priests and rabbis of the South would be some of our strongest allies. Instead, some have been outright opponents, refusing to understand the freedom movement and misrepresenting its leaders; all too many others have been more cautious than courageous and have remained silent behind the anesthetizing security of the stained-glass windows.

In spite of my shattered dreams of the past, I came to Birmingham with the hope that the white religious leadership of this community would see the justice of our cause, and with deep moral concern, serve as the channel through which our just grievances would get to the power structure. I had hoped that each of you would understand. But again I have been disappointed. I have heard numerous religious leaders of the South call upon their worshippers to comply with a desegregation decision because it is the law, but I have longed to hear white ministers say, "Follow this decree because **integration** is morally right and the Negro is your brother." In the midst of blatant injustices inflicted upon the Negro, I have watched white churches stand on the sideline and merely mouth pious irrelevancies and sanctimonious trivialities. In the midst of a mighty struggle to rid our nation of racial and economic injustice, I have heard so many ministers say, "Those are social issues with which the gospel has no real concern," and I have watched so many churches commit themselves to a completely otherworldly religion which made a strange distinction between body and soul, the sacred and the secular.

So here we are moving toward the exit of the twentieth century with a religious community largely adjusted to the status quo, standing as a taillight behind other community agencies rather than a headlight leading men to higher levels of justice....

I must close now. But before closing I am impelled to mention one other point in your statement that troubled me profoundly. You warmly commended the Birmingham police force for keeping "order" and "preventing violence." I don't believe you would have so warmly commended the police force if you had seen its angry violent dogs literally biting six unarmed, nonviolent Negroes. I don't believe you would so quickly commend the policemen if you would observe their ugly and inhuman treatment of Negroes here in the city jail; if you would watch them push and curse old Negro women and young Negro girls; if you would see them slap and kick old Negro men and young boys; if you will observe them, as they did on two occasions, refuse to give us food because we wanted to sing our grace together. I'm sorry that I can't join you in your praise for the police department.

It is true that they have been rather disciplined in their public handling of the demonstrators. In this sense they have been rather publicly "nonviolent." But for what purpose? To preserve the evil system of segregation. Over the last few years I have consistently preached that nonviolence demands that the means we use must be as pure as the ends we seek. So I have tried to make it clear that it is wrong to use immoral means to attain moral ends. But now I must affirm that it is just as wrong, or even more so, to use moral means to preserve immoral ends. Maybe Mr. Connor and his policemen have been rather publicly nonviolent, as **Chief Pritchett** was in Albany,

Integration: The combination of facilities, previously separated by race, into single, multiracial systems.

Pritchett, Laurie: Police chief in Albany, Georgia, in the early 1960s.

Georgia, but they have used the moral means of nonviolence to maintain the immoral end of flagrant racial injustice. **T. S. Eliot** has said that there is no greater treason then to do the right deed for the wrong reason.

I wish you had commended the Negro sit-inners and demonstrators of Birmingham for their **sublime** courage, their willingness to suffer and their amazing discipline in the midst of the most inhuman provocation. One day the South will recognize its real heroes. They will be the **James Merediths**, courageously and with a majestic sense of purpose facing jeering and hostile mobs and the agonizing loneliness that characterizes the life of the pioneer. They will be old, oppressed, battered Negro women, symbolized in a seventy-two-year-old woman of Montgomery, Alabama, who rose up with a sense of dignity and with her people decided not to ride the segregated buses, and responded to one who inquired about her tiredness with ungrammatical profundity: "My feet is tired, but my soul is rested." They will be the young high school and college students, young ministers of the gospel and a host of their elders courageously and nonviolently sitting-in at lunch counters and willingly going to jail for conscience's sake. One day the South will know that when these disinherited children of God sat down at lunch counters they were in reality standing up for the best in the American dream and the most sacred values in our Judeo-Christian heritage, and thusly, carrying our whole nation back to those great wells of democracy which were dug deep by the Founding Fathers in the formulation of the Constitution and the Declaration of Independence.

Never before have I written a letter this long (or should I say a book?). I'm afraid that it is much too long to take your precious time. I can assure you that it would have much shorter if I had been writing from a comfortable desk, but what else is there to do when you are alone for days in the dull monotony of a narrow jail cell other than write long letters, think strange thoughts, and pray long prayers?

If I have said anything in this letter that is an overstatement of the truth and is indicative of an unreasonable impatience, I beg you to forgive me. If I have said anything in this letter that is an understatement of the truth and is indicative of my having patience that makes me patient with anything less than brotherhood, I beg God to forgive me.

I hope this letter finds you strong in the faith. I also hope that circumstances will soon make it possible for me to meet each of you, not as an integrationist or a civil rights leader, but as a fellow clergyman

T. S. Eliot: 1888–1964; Nobel Prize-winning British poet.

Sublime: Supreme or outstanding; awe-inspiring.

James Meredith: The first African American to attend the University of Mississippi, in 1962.

*and a Christian brother. Let us all hope that the dark clouds of racial prejudice will soon pass away and the deep fog of misunderstanding will be lifted from our fear-drenched communities and in some not too distant tomorrow the radiant stars of love and brotherhood will shine over our great nation with all of their **scintillating** beauty.*

Yours for the cause of Peace and Brotherhood,

Martin Luther King Jr.

"I Have a Dream"

I am happy to join with you today in what will go down in history as the greatest demonstration for freedom in the history of our nation.

Fivescore years ago, a great American, in whose symbolic shadow we stand today, signed the Emancipation Proclamation. This momentous decree came as a great beacon of light of hope to millions of Negro slaves who had been seared in the flames of withering injustice. It came as a joyous daybreak to end the long night of their captivity.

*But one hundred years later, the Negro still is not free; one hundred years later, the life of the Negro is still sadly crippled by the **manacles** of segregation and the chains of discrimination; one hundred years later, the Negro lives on a lonely island of poverty in the midst of a vast ocean of material prosperity; one hundred years later, the Negro is still languished in the corners of American society and finds himself in exile in his own land.*

So we've come here today to dramatize a shameful condition. In a sense we've come to our nation's capital to cash a check. When the architects of our republic wrote the magnificent words of the Constitution and the Declaration of Independence, they were signing a promissory note to which every American was to fall heir. This note was the promise that all men, yes, black men as well as white men, would be guaranteed the unalienable rights of life, liberty, and the pursuit of happiness.

It is obvious today that America has defaulted on this promissory note in so far as her citizens of color are concerned. Instead of honoring this sacred obligation, America has given the Negro people a bad check; a check which has come back marked "insufficient funds." We refuse to believe that there are insufficient funds in the great vaults of

Scintillating: Sparkling or twinkling.

Manacle: Handcuff.

Martin Luther King Jr.

Martin Luther King Jr., was born on January 15, 1929, in Atlanta, Georgia, to Martin Luther King Sr., a Baptist minister, and Alberta Williams King, a schoolteacher and a minister's daughter. While attending Morehouse College in Atlanta, King decided that, like his father, he wanted to become a minister. After graduating from Morehouse with a bachelor of arts degree in 1948, King attended Crozer Theological Seminary in Chester, Pennsylvania, and then completed a doctoral program at Boston University.

As a student, King learned about the philosophy of nonviolence of Mohandas (also called Mahatma) Gandhi (1869–1948), the leader of India's independence movement against Great Britain. Like Gandhi, King applied nonviolence to a struggle for social justice—in King's case it was civil rights for African Americans. (Nonviolence is the rejection of all forms of violence. A protest action understaken in the spirit of nonviolence is called passive resistance. Passive resistance is a quiet but firm refusal to comply with unjust laws.)

In 1955, shortly after accepting the position of minister at the Dexter Avenue Baptist Church in Montgomery, Alabama, King was thrust into civil rights activity. He was selected by his fellow black clergymen to head the Montgomery Improvement Association, the group coordinating the Montgomery bus boycott. After 382 days of walking or carpooling, Mongtomery's black populace succeeded in bringing an end to the policy that forced them to sit at the back of the bus and give up their seats for white passengers.

From 1957 to 1968, King presided over the Southern Christian Leadership Conference (SCLC)—an alliance of black ministers and the South's most respected civil rights organization. King's civil rights

opportunity of this nation. And so we've come to cash this check, a check that will give us upon demand the riches of freedom and the security of justice.

We have also come to this hallowed spot to remind America of the fierce urgency of now. This is no time to engage in the luxury of cooling off or to take the tranquilizing drug of gradualism. Now is the time to make real the promises of democracy; now is the time to rise from the dark and desolate valley of segregation to the sunlit path of racial justice; now is the time to lift our nation from the quicksands of racial

Martin Luther King Jr. *Reproduced by permission of American Stock/Archive Photos.*

people to take actions they would have never before imagined possible.

In the final three years of his life, King came to the conclusion that the income gap between rich and poor was every bit as responsible as racial discrimination for the nation's societal ills. He visited northern and western ghettoes and learned that while southern blacks had been victimized by legally sanctioned racial segregation, northern and western blacks suffered from oppressive poverty, overcrowding, and discrimination in housing and employment. In 1966 King led the SCLC into Chicago, to organize slumdwellers around issues of poverty. The following year he made plans for a march by poor people, of all races, on Washington. King did not live to see the Poor People's March. His life was cut short by an assassin's bullet on April 4, 1968, in Memphis, Tennessee.

activities took him to Atlanta and Albany (Georgia), Birmingham and Selma (Alabama), and scores of other cities throughout the South. With his rousing speeches and his willingness to put his body on the line, he inspired thousands of

injustice to the solid rock of brotherhood; now is the time to make justice a reality for all God's children. It would be fatal for the nation to overlook the urgency of the moment. This sweltering summer of the Negro's legitimate discontent will not pass until there is an invigorating autumn of freedom and equality.

Nineteen sixty-three is not an end, but a beginning. And those who hope that the Negro needed to blow off steam and will now be content, will have a rude awakening if the nation returns to business as usual.

There will be neither rest or tranquility in America until the Negro is granted his citizenship rights. The whirlwinds of revolt will continue to shake the foundations of our nation until the bright day of justice emerges.

But there is something that I must say to my people who stand on the warm threshold which leads into the palace of justice. In the process of gaining our rightful place we must not be guilty of wrongful deeds.

Let us not seek to satisfy our thirst for freedom by drinking from the cup of bitterness and hatred. We must forever conduct our struggle on the high plane of dignity and discipline. We must not allow our creative protest to degenerate into physical violence. Again and again we must rise to the majestic heights of meeting physical force with soul force.

*The marvelous new militancy which has engulfed the Negro community must not lead us to a distrust of all white people, for many of our white brothers, as evidenced by their presence here today, have come to realize that their destiny is tied up with our destiny and they have come to realize that their freedom is inextricably bound to our freedom. This offense we share mounted to storm the **battlements** of injustice must be carried forth by a biracial army. We cannot walk alone.*

And as we walk, we must make the pledge that we shall always march ahead. We cannot turn back. There are those who are asking the devotees of civil rights, "When will you be satisfied?" We can never be satisfied as long as the Negro is the victim of the unspeakable horrors of police brutality.

We can never be satisfied as long as our bodies, heavy with fatigue of travel, cannot gain lodging in the motels of the highways and the hotels of the cities. We cannot be satisfied as long as the Negro's basic mobility is from a smaller ghetto to a larger one.

We can never be satisfied as long as our children are stripped of their selfhood and robbed of their dignity by signs stating "for whites only." We cannot be satisfied as long as a Negro in Mississippi cannot vote and a Negro in New York believes he has nothing for which to vote. No, we are not satisfied, and we will not be satisfied until justice rolls down like the waters and righteousness like a mighty stream.

I am not unmindful that some of you have come here out of excessive trials and tribulation. Some of you have come fresh from

Battlements: A wall used as protection or for concealment.

narrow jail cells. Some of you have come from areas where your quest for freedom left you battered by the storms of persecution and staggered by the winds of police brutality. You have been the veterans of creative suffering. Continue to work with the faith that unearned suffering is redemptive.

Go back to Mississippi; go back to Alabama; go back to South Carolina; go back to Georgia; go back to Louisiana; go back to the slums and ghettos of the northern cities, knowing that somehow this situation can, and will be changed. Let us not wallow in the valley of despair.

So I say to you, my friends, that even though we must face the difficulties of today and tomorrow, I still have a dream. It is a dream deeply rooted in the American dream that one day this nation will rise up and live out the true meaning of its creed—we hold these truths to be self-evident, that all men are created equal.

I have a dream that one day on the red hills of Georgia, sons of former slaves and sons of former slave-owners will be able to sit down together at the table of brotherhood.

I have a dream that one day, even the state of Mississippi, a state sweltering with the heat of injustice, sweltering with the heat of oppression, will be transformed into an oasis of freedom and justice.

I have a dream my four little children will one day live in a nation where they will not be judged by the color of their skin but by the content of their character. I have a dream today!

*I have a dream that one day, down in Alabama, with its vicious racists, and its governor having his lips dripping with the words of interposition and **nullification**, that one day, right there in Alabama, little black boys and black girls will be able to join hands with little white boys and white girls as sisters and brothers. I have a dream today!*

*I have a dream that one day every valley shall be **exalted**, every hill and mountain shall be made low, the rough places shall be made plain, and the crooked places shall be made straight and the glory of the Lord will be revealed and all flesh shall see it together.*

This is our hope. This is the faith that I go back to the South with.

With this faith we will be able to hear out of the mountain of despair a stone of hope. With this faith we will be able to transform the jangling discords of our nation into a beautiful symphony of brotherhood.

Nullification: To make something ineffective.

Exalted: Elevated in rank, honor, or power.

With this faith we will be able to work together, to pray together, to struggle together, to go to jail together, to stand up for freedom together, knowing that we will be free one day. This will be the day when all of God's children will be able to sing with new meaning—"my country 'tis of thee; sweet land of liberty; of thee I sing; land where my fathers died, land of the pilgrim's pride; from every mountain side, let freedom ring"—and if America is to be a great nation, this must become true.

So let freedom ring from the **prodigious** hilltops of New Hampshire.

Let freedom ring from the mighty mountains of New York.

Let freedom ring from the heightening Alleghenies of Pennsylvania.

Let freedom ring from the snow-capped Rockies of Colorado.

Let freedom ring from the curvaceous slopes of California.

But not only that.

Let freedom ring from Stone Mountain of Georgia.

Let freedom ring from Lookout Mountain of Tennessee.

Let freedom ring from every hill and molehill of Mississippi, from every mountainside, let freedom ring.

And when we allow freedom to ring, when we let it ring from every village and hamlet, from every state and city, we will be able to speed up that day when all of God's children—black men and white men, Jews and Gentiles, Catholics and Protestants—will be able to join hands and to sing in the worlds of the old Negro spiritual, "Free at last, free at last; thank God Almighty, we are free at last." (Washington, pp. 217–20, 289–302)

Prodigious: Extraordinary, wonderful, or marvelous.

What happened next...

The hopefulness that characterized the March on Washington was short-lived. On Sunday, September 15, just eighteen days after the March on Washington, a bomb was set off in Birmingham's Sixteenth Street Baptist Church, killing four young girls. The victims were Denise McNair, age eleven;

and Cynthia Wesley, Carole Robertson, and Addie Mae Collins, all age fourteen. Twenty-one people were injured in the bombing; one of the victims, a ten-year-old girl, was critically injured.

Two months later, on November 22, 1963, President John F. Kennedy was gunned down in Dallas, Texas. Many people feared that without Kennedy to champion the civil rights bill, it had little chance of passing. Fortunately, Kennedy's successor—Lyndon B. Johnson (1908–1973)—made the passage of the civil rights bill his top priority. He signed the 1964 Civil Rights Act into law on July 2, 1964.

The Civil Rights Act of 1964 was the most expansive civil rights policy in American history. It prohibited discrimination in employment, voting, public accommodations (such as restaurants, hotels, stores, libraries, swimming pools, parks, and theaters), and education. The legislation also mandated the desegregation of public schools and banned discrimination in selecting participants for federally funded programs (such as worker training programs and welfare).

President John F. Kennedy introduced his civil rights bill to Congress on June 19, 1963. After Kennedy's assassination, the bill was signed by his successor, Lyndon B. Johnson, in 1964. *Reproduced by permission of the Library of Congress.*

One area that the 1964 Civil Rights Act did not adequately address was voting rights. King and other civil rights leaders next set their sights on federal legislation that would outlaw the variety of practices (such as the literacy test, which required prospective black registrants to read and interpret a section of the state constitution to the satisfaction of the registrar, and poll taxes) used by white officials to keep blacks from voting. To dramatize their cause, civil rights leaders organized a major voting-rights campaign in Selma, Alabama—a city in which the majority of the citizens were black, yet less than 3 percent of black adults were registered to vote.

In January and February 1965, thousands of Selma residents were arrested, and many were beaten, in demonstrations at the courthouse. King and other SCLC leaders planned to hold a fifty-four-mile-long march from Selma to the state capital of Montgomery, to present their grievances to Alabama's racist governor George C. Wallace. The march began on March 7, a day later remembered as "Bloody Sunday." Hundreds of marchers were beaten mercilessly by local police and state troopers on the Edmund Pettus Bridge at the edge of Selma. After a second abortive attempt to leave Selma, the marchers were finally allowed to proceed. On March 29, 25,000 marchers triumphantly strode up to the capitol building in Montgomery.

Although President Johnson had stated in late 1964 that he would introduce no new civil rights legislation in 1965, the events in Selma led him to change his mind. In March 1965 Johnson presented Congress with a voting rights bill that would outlaw all practices used to deny blacks the right to vote and would empower federal registrars to register black voters. The 1965 Voting Rights Act passed on August 6, 1965. Shortly thereafter, the number of black voters surged dramatically throughout the South.

King then shifted his emphasis to economic rights for all poor Americans, regardless of race. He also became an outspoken critic of the Vietnam War (1954–75), from the point of view of one who shuns violence. He railed against the high level of spending on the war at the expense of social programs and the disproportionate number of poor people and racial minorities dying in the conflict. In April 1968, while in Memphis, Tennessee, supporting a strike by African American sanitation workers, King was shot to death. Eighteen years later, a national holiday was established in King's honor.

Did you know...

- In 1963 King was chosen as "Man of the Year" by *Time* Magazine. In 1964, King received an even higher honor—the Nobel Peace Prize.

- King was persuaded to form the Southern Christian Leadership Conference in 1957 by Ella Baker (1903–1986), then a fifty-two-year-old civil rights activist from New York. Baker believed that black ministers could inspire large numbers of people to become involved in the civil rights movement.

- King was arrested in a demonstration at a racially segregated lunch counter in Atlanta, Georgia, on October 19, 1960, and sentenced to four months of hard labor at the notorious Reidsville State Prison. His sentence was commuted by the judge at the urging of Robert F. Kennedy (1925–1968), then the campaign manager (and later attorney general) for his brother, presidential candidate John F. Kennedy. Kennedy took 68 percent of the black vote in the following month's election and defeated opponent Richard Nixon by a very narrow margin.

- In the fall of 1958, during a book signing at a New York City bookstore for his newly published *Stride Toward Freedom*, King was attacked by a woman in the crowd. The woman stabbed King in the chest with a letter opener, proclaiming "I've been after him for six years! I'm glad I done it!" King nearly died from his injury. In order to remove the blade, which just missed his heart, doctors had to removed two of King's ribs.

For More Information See

Books and Pamphlets

Speeches By the Leaders: The March on Washington for Jobs and Freedom (pamphlet). New York: NAACP, 1963.

Why We Can't Wait. New York: Harper & Row, 1963.

Sources

Books

African American Biography. Vol. 3. Detroit: U•X•L, 1994, pp. 456–59.

Branch, Taylor. *Parting the Waters: America in the King Years, 1957–1963.* New York: Simon & Schuster, Inc., 1988.

Garrow, David J. *Protest at Selma: Martin Luther King, Jr., and the Voting Rights Act of 1965.* New Haven, CT: Yale University Press, 1978.

Lewis, John. *Walking With the Wind.* New York: Simon & Schuster, 1998.

Salmond, John A. *My Mind Set on Freedom: A History of the Civil Rights Movement, 1954–1968.* Chicago: Ivan R. Dee, 1997.

Washington, James Melvin, ed. *A Testament of Hope: The Essential Writings of Martin Luther King, Jr.* San Francisco: Harper & Row, 1986.

Williams, Juan. *Eyes on the Prize: America's Civil Rights Years, 1954–1965.* New York: Penguin Books, 1987.

Other

Eyes on the Prize: America's Civil Rights Years (videocassette; six episodes). Boston: Blackside, Inc., 1986.

Eyes on the Prize II: America at the Racial Crossroads—1965–1985 (videocassette; six episodes). Boston: Blackside, Inc., 1989.

John Robert Lewis

Original text of speech at the March on Washington for Jobs and Freedom

Written in 1963
Reprinted in *Walking with the Wind:*
A Memoir of the Movement
Published in 1988

John Lewis was the twenty-three-year-old national chairman of the Student Nonviolent Coordinating Committee (SNCC; pronounced "snick") when he spoke before 250,000 people at the August 28, 1963, March on Washington for Jobs and Freedom. Lewis, who grew up picking cotton alongside his parents and siblings in rural Pike County, Alabama, had developed a keen interest in religion and social justice during his youth. In 1960, while attending seminary in Nashville, Tennessee, he became a leader of the student sit-in movement. Soon thereafter he joined the SNCC and went to work with the organization's desegregation and voter registration programs all over the South. He was elected the SNCC's national chairman in 1963, a position he held until 1966.

From 1960 to 1963, the years preceding the March on Washington, Lewis and other members of the SNCC were engaged in difficult, dangerous work in the most segregated regions of the South. For their efforts to integrate public accommodations (such as restaurants, bus terminals, and libraries) and register African American voters, SNCC workers were subjected to arrests, beatings, shootings, bombings, and even killings. The

"In the struggle, we must seek more than civil rights; we must work for the community of love, peace and true brotherhood. Our minds, souls and hearts cannot rest until freedom and justice exist for *all people.*"

On March 7, 1965, John Lewis (front right) leads marchers out of Selma, Alabama, on the way to Montgomery, Alabama. As chairman of the SNCC from 1963 to 1966, Lewis worked on the organization's desegregation and voter registration programs all over the South.
Reproduced by permission of AP/Wide World Photos.

SNCC, more than any other civil rights organization at the time, was truly in the trenches of the battle for racial justice.

Since the SNCC's inception, relations were strained between the student organization and other, more established, civil rights organizations—primarily the Southern Christian Leadership Conference (SCLC) and the National Association for the Advancement of Colored People (NAACP). SNCC members felt that the SCLC and the NAACP were too cautious and conservative in their efforts; furthermore, the SNCC resented the fact that the established groups garnered a disproportionate amount of publicity and funding. For their part, the older activist guard felt that the SNCC was too radical and strident and worried that the organization would upset the tenuous relationship between the civil rights community and the federal government.

John Lewis, however, had a foot in both camps. Throughout his years as the SNCC's chairman, he also served on

the board of the SCLC. And when other SNCC members accused Martin Luther King Jr. (president of the SCLC; 1929–1968) of softening his stance to placate white America or of claiming credit for achievements that had come about largely due to the efforts of the SNCC, Lewis hailed King as a civil rights hero.

In June 1963 Lewis was among the leaders of the "big six" civil rights organizations that came together to plan a

News commentators at the 1963 March on Washington. On August 28, John Lewis delivered one of the march's most forceful speeches. *Reproduced by permission of the National Archives and Records Administration.*

march in the nation's capital. (The other leaders included King; A. Philip Randolph, founder of the Brotherhood of Sleeping Car Porters; Roy Wilkins, president of the NAACP; James Farmer, chairman of the Congress on Racial Equality; and Whitney Young, president of the National Urban League.) The purpose of the march was to show support for the sweeping civil rights bill proposed by President John F. Kennedy (1917–1963). That bill, which was signed into law one year later by President Lyndon B. Johnson (1908–1973) as the 1964 Civil Rights Act, spelled an end to segregation of all public accommodations and a shorter timetable for school desegregation.

Lewis was one of a handful of political leaders scheduled to deliver speeches at the Lincoln Memorial, the end point of the march. He worked on his speech during the week leading up to the march, assisted by several of his SNCC colleagues. The final version of Lewis's written speech, as it is excerpted, reflected the justifiable anger and frustrations of the SNCC's beleaguered field workers.

The night before the march, Lewis was notified that some of the other march leaders felt his speech was too forceful. They were concerned that it would shatter the fragile unity of the civil rights groups that had coalesced around the march and hurt the civil rights bill's chances of passage. Only under pressure from Randolph, the elder statesman of the civil rights movement, did Lewis agree to soften his text. Lewis—together with Randolph, march staffer Bayard Rustin, King, and Reverend Eugene Carson Blake of the National Council of Churches—hastily gathered behind the statue of Abraham Lincoln and hashed out last minute changes to the speech. At the same time, more than 250,000 people stood in front of the Lincoln Memorial listening to songs and speeches.

Things to remember while reading John Lewis's speech:

- This is *original text* of Lewis's speech, not the version he actually delivered at the Lincoln Memorial. Among the passages Lewis deleted from his prepared text were the description of Kennedy's civil rights bill as "too little and too late"; the command to "march through the heart of Dixie, the way Sherman did"; the question "which side is the federal government on?"; and the adjective "cheap" in reference to political leaders.

- Lewis speaks of three protesters in Americus, Georgia, facing the death penalty for nonviolent actions. (A protest action understaken in the spirit of nonviolence is called passive resistance. Passive resistance is a quiet but firm refusal to comply with unjust laws.) Those three men— SNCC workers Don Harris, Ralph Allen, and John Perdew—had been arrested during a civil rights demonstration in southwestern Georgia. Harris let his body go limp and was jolted by a policeman's electric cattle prod. That action provoked some onlookers to throw bricks at the police; the police retaliated by firing bullets into the crowd. Harris, Allen, and Perdew were charged with seditious conspiracy (attempting to overthrow the government), a charge punishable by death.

- Lewis makes reference to Danville, Virginia, one of the more than 100 cities throughout the South where desegregation campaigns took place in the summer of 1963. Danville made headlines when police kicked down the door of a black church and assaulted sixty-five meeting participants with firehoses and clubs.

- Lewis points to the abuse and arrests of African Americans in Albany as examples of the hazards of working for civil rights. He mentions C. B. King, a black attorney representing a jailed SNCC member, who was beaten over the head by a sheriff. He also brings up Marion King—the pregnant wife of local protest leader Slater King (C. B. King's brother)—who was beaten and kicked by a deputy sheriff and subsequently suffered a miscarriage.

Original text of John Lewis's speech at March on Washington for Jobs and Freedom

We march today for jobs and freedom, but we have nothing to be proud of, for hundreds and thousands of our brothers are not here.

They have no money for their transportation, for they are receiving starvation wages, or no wages at all.

In good conscience, we cannot support wholeheartedly the administration's civil rights bill, for it is too little and too late. There's not one thing in the bill that will protect our people from police brutality.

This bill will not protect young children and old women from police dogs and fire hoses, for engaging in peaceful demonstrations. This bill will not protect the citizens in Danville, Virginia, who must live in constant fear in a police state. This bill will not protect the hundreds of people who have been arrested on trumped-up charges. What about the three young men in Americus, Georgia, who face the death penalty for engaging in peaceful protest?

The voting section of this bill will not help thousands of black citizens who want to vote. It will not help the citizens of Mississippi, of Alabama and Georgia, who are qualified to vote but lack a sixth-grade education. "ONE MAN, ONE VOTE" is the African cry. It is ours, too. It must be ours.

People have been forced to leave their homes because they dared to exercise their right to register to vote. What is there in this bill to ensure the equality of a maid who earns $5 a week in the home of a family whose income is $100,000 a year?

*For the first time in one hundred years this nation is being awakened to the fact that **segregation** is evil and that it must be destroyed in all forms. Your presence today proves that you have been aroused to the point of action.*

*We are now involved in a serious revolution. This nation is still a place of cheap political leaders who build their careers on immoral compromises and ally themselves with open forms of political, economic and social exploitation. What political leader here can stand up and say, "My party is the party of principles?" The party of Kennedy is also the party of **Eastland**. The party of **Javits** is also the party of **Goldwater**.*

Where is our party?

In some parts of the South we work in the fields from sunup to sundown for $12 a week. In Albany, Georgia, nine of our leaders have been indicted not by Dixiecrats but by the federal government for peaceful protest. But what did the federal government do when Albany's deputy sheriff beat attorney C. B. King and left him half dead? What did the federal government do when local police officials kicked and assaulted the pregnant wife of Slater King, and she lost her baby?

Segregation: The separation of the races, as dictated by laws and social customs.

James O. Eastland: 1904–1986; diehard white supremacist senator from Mississippi; served in 1941 and from 1943–1978.

Jacob Javits: 1904–1986; liberal senator from New York, serving from 1957 through 1980.

Barry Goldwater: 1909–1998; conservative senator from Arizona for five terms, from 1953 through 1964, and from 1969 through 1986.

It seems to me that the Albany indictment is part of a conspiracy on the part of the federal government and local politicians in the interest of expediency.

I want to know, which side is the federal government on?

The revolution is at hand, and we must free ourselves of the chains of political and economic slavery. The nonviolent revolution is saying, "We will not wait for the court to act, for we have been waiting for hundreds of years. We will not wait for the President, the Justice Department, nor Congress, but we will take matters into our own hands and create a source of power, outside of any national structure, that could and would assure us a victory."

To those who have said, "Be patient and wait," we must say that "patience" is a dirty and nasty word. We cannot be patient, we do not want to be free gradually. We want our freedom, and we want it now. *We cannot depend on any political party, for both the Democrats and the Republicans have betrayed the basic principles of the Declaration of Independence.*

We all recognize the fact that if any radical social, political and economic changes are to take place in our society, the people, the masses, must bring them about. In the struggle, we must seek more than civil rights; we must work for the community of love, peace and true brotherhood. Our minds, souls and hearts cannot rest until free-dom and justice exist for all people.

The revolution is a serious one. Mr. Kennedy is trying to take the revolution out of the streets and put it into the courts. Listen, Mr. Kennedy. Listen, Mr. Congressman. Listen, fellow citizens. The black masses are on the march for jobs and freedom, and we must say to the politicians that there won't be a "cooling-off" period.

All of us must get in the revolution. Get in and stay in the streets of every city, every village and every hamlet of this nation until true free-dom comes, until the revolution is complete. In the Delta of Mississippi, in southwest Georgia, in Alabama, Harlem, Chicago, Detroit, Philadel-phia and all over this nation, the black masses are on the march!

We won't stop now. All of the forces of Eastland, **Barnett, Wal-lace** *and* **Thurmond** *won't stop this revolution. The time will come when we will not confine our marching to Washington. We will march through the South, through the heart of Dixie, the way* **Sherman** *did. We shall pursue our own "scorched earth" policy and burn* **Jim Crow** *to the ground—nonviolently. We shall fragment the South into a*

Ross Barnett: died in 1987; segregationist governor of Mississippi in the 1960s.

George Wallace: 1919–1998; governor of Alabama from 1963–1967, 1971–1978, and 1983–1987. A staunch segregationist during the 1960s, Wallace denounced his racist beliefs later in life.

Strom Thurmond: 1902– ; conservative senator from South Carolina, serving from 1954 to the present. Opposed integration in the 1960s.

William Tecumseh Sherman: 1820–1891; Union general during the American Civil War (1861–1865).

Jim Crow: A network of laws and customs that dictated the separation of the races on every level of society.

 **John Lewis**

John Lewis was born on February 21, 1940, in Pike County, Alabama. He was the third of ten children born to sharecropper parents. (Sharecropping is a system of farming in which a landless farmer works a plot of land and in return gives the landowner a share of the crop.) Lewis developed an early interest in religion and, as a teenager, was inspired by a radio broadcast of a sermon given by Martin Luther King Jr.

After high school, Lewis enrolled in the American Baptist Theological Seminary in Nashville, Tennessee. While a student he attended workshops on nonviolence and became active in a newly formed civil rights group, the Nashville Student Movement. In 1960 Lewis and his friends participated in lunch counter sit-ins. (Sit-ins were a form of civil rights protest in which black students, sometimes joined by white students, would request service at segregated lunch counters, then refuse to leave when denied service.)

In April 1960 members of the student sit-in movement from all over the South came together to form the Student Nonviolent Coordinating Committee (SNCC; pronounced "snick"). Based on the principles of nonviolence, integration, and racial equality, the SNCC's goal was to achieve racial equality at all levels of society. Lewis joined the SNCC shortly after the group's formation. He spent the next six years working with the SNCC's desegregation and voting rights campaigns in numerous rural and urban southern locations, and served as the SNCC's national chairman from 1963 until 1966.

During the first half of the 1960s, Lewis participated in several well-publicized efforts to further the cause of civil rights. In 1961 Lewis embarked on the

thousand pieces and put them back together in the image of democracy. We will make the action of the past few months look petty. And I say to you, WAKE UP AMERICA! (Lewis, pp. 216–18)

What happened next...

On Sunday, September 15, just eighteen days after the

John Lewis. *Reproduced by permission of AP/Wide World Photos.*

Freedom Rides—journeys throughout the South by integrated groups of people, to test the enforcement of a pair of Supreme Court rulings striking down the constitutionality of segregated seating on interstate (crossing state lines) buses and trains, as well as segregation in terminal waiting rooms, rest rooms, and restaurants. Two years later, Lewis worked with members of other civil rights organizations to coordinate the March on Washington for Jobs and Freedom. And in 1965, while leading hundreds of people over Selma, Alabama's, Edmund Pettus Bridge en route to Montgomery, Lewis had his head cracked open by a police officer's club.

In 1980 Lewis began his foray into electoral politics. His first victory was to the city council of Atlanta. In 1986 Lewis captured the congressional seat from the Georgia district including Atlanta. Today, serving his seventh term in the U.S. House of Representatives, Lewis continues to fight for social justice.

March on Washington, the euphoria that had surrounded the march was shattered. On that date a bomb was detonated in Birmingham's Sixteenth Street Baptist Church, killing four young girls and injuring twenty-one other people.

Tragedy struck again on November 22, 1963, with the assassination of President John F. Kennedy. Kennedy had been the driving force behind the passage of the civil rights bill; with his death the legislation appeared to be in jeopardy. Fortunately, Kennedy's successor Lyndon B. Johnson doggedly pursued the passage of the civil rights bill. On July 2, 1964, Johnson signed the 1964 Civil Rights Act into law.

The Civil Rights Act of 1964 was the most comprehensive civil rights legislation in the history of the United States. It banned discrimination in employment, voting, public accommodations (such as restaurants, hotels, stores, libraries, swimming pools, parks, and theaters), and education. The act also required the desegregation of public schools and prohibited discrimination in the selection of participants in federally funded programs (such as worker training programs and welfare).

In the summer of 1964, while Johnson was busy lining up votes for the Civil Rights Act, John Lewis was helping coordinate Freedom Summer—the SNCC's massive voter registration project in Mississippi. SNCC recruited upwards of 1,000 college students, mostly whites from prestigious northern colleges, to fan out through the countryside convincing local people to attempt to register to vote. Freedom Summer volunteers also established community centers, health clinics, legal clinics, community feeding sites called "freedom kitchens," and "freedom schools" for African American children.

As 1964 drew to a close, many members of the SNCC were rethinking their commitment to nonviolence. The beatings and intimidation they had endured had taken a huge physical and emotional toll. Many SNCC members came to the conclusion that practicing nonviolence in the South was like speaking a foreign language, and some began carrying weapons. There was also a growing trend toward separatism (the rejection of white culture and institutions, in favor of separate African American culture and institutions).

Lewis was not among those people who shunned nonviolence and embraced separatism. He held fast to his concept of a "beloved community," a society that is truly integrated, nonviolent, and economically just. The differences between Lewis and others in the SNCC grew over the next two years, culminating in Lewis's removal from the helm of the organization in 1966.

Did you know...
- Throughout his career as a civil rights activist, Lewis was arrested more than forty times for nonviolent actions.

- Lewis endured so many beatings at the hands of racist officials and mobs that his head still bears scars and dents. He received one of his earliest beatings on the first leg of the Freedom Rides, in Rock Hill, South Carolina, as he attempted to enter the terminal's "whites-only" restroom. Later during the Freedom Rides, in Montgomery, Alabama, Lewis was beaten unconscious by a white mob. His bloodied face was pictured in major daily newspapers around the world. Lewis's most severe beating, from which he suffered a concussion and a fractured skull, came at the hands of state troopers on the Edmund Pettus Bridge on March 8, 1965, during the Selma-to-Montgomery march.

- Lewis was outspoken in his opposition to the Vietnam War (1954–75). He was especially critical of the disproportionate number of African American fatalities in the war (while blacks comprised only 10 percent of the U.S. population, they comprised 25 percent of fatalities in Vietnam). In December 1965 Lewis was granted the status of "conscientious objector" and exempted from military service. After Lewis authored and released an antiwar statement on behalf of the SNCC, calling on young people to refuse the draft, his status was changed to "morally unfit for service."

- In recent years, as a congressman, Lewis has opposed U.S. involvement in the Persian Gulf War (January to February 1991) and has resisted federal efforts to expand the death penalty. He also refused to participate in the Million Man March in Washington, D.C., on October 16, 1995. He denounced the march's initiator—Louis Farrakhan (1933–), the controversial minister of the separatist black Muslim group Nation of Islam—as a bigot.

Sources

Books

Carson, Clayborne. *In Struggle: SNCC and the Black Awakening of the 1960s.* Cambridge: Harvard University Press, 1981.

Levy, Peter B. *The Civil Rights Movement.* Westwood, CT: Greenwood Press, 1998.

Lewis, John. *Walking with the Wind.* New York: Simon and Schuster, 1998.

Salmond, John A. *My Mind Set on Freedom: A History of the Civil Rights Movement, 1954–1968.* Chicago: Ivan R. Dee, 1997.

Williams, Juan. *Eyes on the Prize: America's Civil Rights Years, 1954–1965.* New York: Penguin Books, 1987.

Periodicals

Wilentz, Sean. "The Last Integrationist: John Lewis's American Odyssey." *New Republic.* July 1, 1996: 19+.

Fannie Lou Hamer

"Everybody Knows about Mississippi, God Damn"

Excerpt from *This Little Light of Mine:*
The Life of Fannie Lou Hamer
Published in 1993

When Fannie Lou Hamer became involved with the civil rights movement in 1962 she was a forty-four-year-old agricultural worker from rural Mississippi. Hamer had heard that young people from the Student Nonviolent Coordinating Committee (SNCC; pronounced "snick") were in the area, trying to help locals register to vote. Before that time, Hamer had not even realized that African Americans were legally entitled to vote. On August 30, 1962, she attended a voter registration meeting to see for herself what all the discussion was about. Hamer was immediately drawn to the activists' message. She signed up to go to the Sunflower County courthouse the next day to attempt to become a registered voter.

Members of the SNCC, led by a young Harvard-educated teacher named Robert Moses (1935–), had been conducting voter registration work in Mississippi since 1961. The work was extremely dangerous, and the results were almost too meager to measure.

Mississippi, nicknamed the "closed society," was undeniably the most segregated state in the United States. While African Americans made up 45 percent of the population in

"[Is] this America, the land of the free and the home of the brave where we have to sleep with our telephones off the hooks because our lives be threatened daily because we want to live as decent human beings, in America?"

Mississippi, in 1960 only 5 percent of all blacks in the state were registered to vote. Blacks were prevented from registering to vote by Jim Crow laws (primary among them being the literacy test), economic intimidation (such as threats of job loss), and outright violence. Mississippi had the South's greatest number of lynchings, beatings, and unexplained disappearances of black residents.

When Hamer became involved in the voter registration campaign, she discovered firsthand the consequences of fighting for her rights. Upon returning from the courthouse (where she and seventeen other applicants had failed the literacy test), Hamer was evicted from her home of eighteen years. She then moved into the home of a friend in the nearby town of Ruleville. Ten days later an attempt was made on Hamer's life when sixteen shots were fired into her friend's window.

Despite the harassment and intimidation, Hamer pressed on. "The only thing they could to me was kill me," stated Hamer, "and it seemed like they'd been trying to do that a little bit at a time ever since I could remember." Hamer joined the staff of the SNCC and leaped into the voter registration campaign with both feet. Before long she had earned a reputation as the "angriest woman in Mississippi."

In the summer of 1964 the SNCC recruited 1,000 volunteers, most of them white students from elite northern colleges, to conduct civil rights work in Mississippi. Some of the students fanned out through the countryside convincing local people to attempt to register to vote, while others operated community centers, health clinics, legal clinics, community feeding sites called "freedom kitchens," and "freedom schools" for African American children.

Moses coordinated volunteer efforts to build a new political party, the Mississippi Freedom Democratic Party (MFDP). The MFDP was organized in accordance with official Democratic Party rules. Its purpose was to serve as an alternative to the regular Democratic Party, which excluded blacks. The MFDP signed up 80,000 members in time for the party's August 6 statewide convention. At that gathering they elected sixty-eight delegates to attend the upcoming national Democratic Party convention in Atlantic City, New Jersey. Hamer was chosen to be the MFDP's vice-chairperson.

Members of the Mississippi Freedom Democratic Party at the 1964 Democratic Party national convention in Atlantic City, New Jersey. *Reproduced by permission of AP/Wide World Photos.*

On August 24 the MFDP delegates arrived at the national convention and asked to be seated in place of the regular Democrats. MFDP delegates argued that their party was much more representative of the people of Mississippi than was the regular Democratic party. Freedom Party delegates also pointed out that they, unlike the regular Democrats, were loyal to the national Democratic Party candidates and platform. (During the civil rights era, the Republican Party was virtually nonexistent in the South. Southern Democrats typically sided with northern Republicans in Congress.)

The convention's credentials committee was responsible for deciding which Mississippi delegation to recognize. Several MFDP representatives testified before the committee. They described how blacks were excluded from participating in the regular Democratic Party, as well as the overall wretched conditions for blacks in Mississippi. The day's most powerful testimony was delivered by Hamer.

Things to remember while reading the excerpt from "Everybody Knows about Mississippi, God Damn:"

- The beginning of Hamer's speech was carried live on national television. President Lyndon B. Johnson (1908–1973), attempting to prevent a rift in the Democratic Party that might jeopardize his nomination for a second term as president, called an impromptu press conference to divert media attention. Hamer's speech was aired later that evening, provoking thousands of people to send the credentials committee telegrams supporting the MFDP.

- In her testimony, Hamer mentioned the arrest of a bus driver for driving a "bus of wrong color." The bus she referred to was an old school bus that had been rented by the SNCC in August 1962 to take Hamer and seventeen other African Americans to the county seat in Indianola, to try to register to vote. On the way back to Ruleville, the driver had been pulled over and charged with driving a bus that was "too yellow" and that could be confused with a school bus. The group had chipped in to pay the $35 fine so they could continue to Ruleville.

- When Hamer stated "I question America," she summed up the sentiments of thousands of civil rights workers who had been doggedly struggling for rights to which African Americans were already legally entitled. In the years preceding the convention it had become painfully obvious that the federal government—the body charged with protecting American lives and freedoms—was turning a blind eye to the injustices confronting black citizens. For many activists, the formation of the MFDP represented a final, good-faith effort to work within the political system.

"Everybody Knows about Mississippi, God Damn"

The following excerpt presents Fannie Lou Hamer's testimony before the Democratic Party's credentials committee, August 22, 1964.

Mr. Chairman, and the Credentials Committee, my name is Mrs. Fannie Lou Hamer, and I live at 626 East Lafayette Street, Ruleville, Mississippi, Sunflower County, the home of Senator **James O. Eastland,** *and* **Senator Stennis.**

It was the 31st of August in 1962 that eighteen of us traveled twenty-six miles to the county courthouse in Indianola to try to register to try to become first-class citizens. We was met in Indianola by Mississippi men, highway patrolmens, and they only allowed two of us in to take the **literacy test** *at the time. After we had taken this test and started back to Ruleville, we was held up by the City Police and the State Highway Patrolmen and carried back to Indianola, where the bus driver was charged that day with driving a bus the wrong color.*

After we paid the fine among us, we continued on to Ruleville, and Reverend Jeff Sunny carried me four miles in the rural area where I had worked as a **timekeeper** *and* **sharecropper** *for eighteen years. I was met there by my children, who told me the plantation owner was angry because I had gone down to try to register. After they told me, my husband came, and said the plantation owner was raising cain because I had tried to register, and before he quit talking the plantation owner came, and said, "Fannie Lou, do you know—did Pap tell you what I said?"*

I said, "Yes, sir."

He said, "I mean that," he said. "If you don't go down and withdraw your registration, you will have to leave," said, "Then if you go down and withdraw," he said. "You will—you might have to go because we are not ready for that in Mississippi."

James O. Eastland: 1904–1986; diehard white supremacist senator from Mississippi; served in 1941 and from 1943–1978.

Senator Stennis: John Stennis; segregationist U.S. Senator from Mississippi in the 1960s.

Literacy test: Selectively administered to black applicants, the test required would-be voters to read and/or interpret a section of the state constitution to the satisfaction of the registrar.

Timekeeper: One who keeps track of agricultural workers' hours and informs them when it is starting time, break time, and quitting time.

Sharecropper: A landless farmer who works a plot of land and in return gives the landowner a share of the crop.

And I addressed him and told him and said, "I didn't try to register for you. I tried to register for myself." I had to leave that same night.

On the 10th of September, 1962, sixteen bullets was fired into the home of Mr. and Mrs. Robert Tucker for me. That same night two girls were shot in Ruleville, Mississippi. Also Mr. Joe McDonald's house was shot in.

And in June, the 9th, 1963, I had attended a voter-registration workshop, was returning back to Mississippi. Ten of us traveling by the Continental Trailway bus. When we got to Winona, Mississippi, which is Montgomery County, four of the people got off to use the washroom, and two of the people—to use the restaurant—two of the people wanted to use the washroom. The four people that had gone in to use the restaurant was ordered out. During this time I was on the bus. But when I looked through the window and saw they had rushed out, I got off of the bus to see what had happened, and one of the ladies said, "It was a state highway patrolman and a chief of police ordered us out."

I got back on the bus and one of the persons had used the washroom got back on the bus, too. As soon as I was seated on the bus, I saw when they began to get the four people in a highway patrolman's car. I stepped off the bus to see what was happening and somebody screamed from the car that the four workers was in and said, "Get that one there," and when I went to get in the car, when the man told me I was under arrest, he kicked me.

I was carried to the county jail, and put in the booking room. They left some of the people in the booking room and began to place us in cells, I was placed in a cell with a young woman called Miss Euvester Simpson. After I was placed in the cell I began to hear sounds of licks and screams. I could hear the sounds of licks and horrible screams, and I could hear somebody say, "Can you say, yes sir, nigger? Can you say yes, sir?"

And they would say other horrible names. She would say, "Yes, I can say yes, sir."

"So say it."

She says, "I don't know you well enough."

They beat her, I don't know how long, and after a while she began to pray, and asked God to have mercy on those people.

And it wasn't too long before three white men came to my cell. One

Fannie Lou Hamer

Fannie Lou Hamer was born in 1917 in Montgomery County, Mississippi, the youngest of twenty children of sharecropper parents. When Hamer was two years old, her family moved to a plantation in the flat Delta lands of Sunflower County—the county she was to call home for the rest of her life.

Hamer's family worked hard in the fields day in and day out, with little to show for it. At one point the family saved enough money to buy some livestock, with the dream of starting their own farm. The white landowners quickly extinguished that dream by poisoning the animals.

Hamer toiled in the fields until the age of forty-four. A turning point in her life came in August 1962, when she attended a voter registration meeting. Hamer then attempted to register to vote, only to lose her home and her job as retribution. Hamer remained undeterred and continued her civil rights activities, even after she was severely beaten in jail and

Fannie Lou Hamer. *Reproduced by permission of UPI/Bettmann.*

received numerous death threats. Hamer became one of the civil rights movement's most forceful organizers and most eloquent spokespersons. Until her death in 1977, Hamer devoted all her energies to fighting for the political and economic rights of poor people and people of color.

---

of these men was a State Highway Patrolman and he asked me where I was from, and I told him Ruleville. He said, "We are going to check this." And they left my cell and it wasn't too long before they came back. He said, "You are from Ruleville all right," and he used a curse word, and he said, "We are going to make you wish you was dead."

*I was carried out of that cell into another cell where they had two Negro prisoners. The State Highway Patrolman ordered the first Negro to take the **blackjack**.*

Blackjack: A weapon consisting of a piece of leather-enclosed metal with a strap for a handle.

The first Negro prisoner ordered me, by orders from the State Highway Patrolman for me, to lay down on a bunk bed on my face, and I laid on my face. The first Negro began to beat, and I was beat by the first Negro until he was exhausted, and I was holding my hands behind me at that time on my left side because I suffered from polio when I was six years old. After the first Negro had beat until he was exhausted, the State Highway Patrolman ordered the second Negro to take the blackjack.

The second Negro began to beat and I began to work my feet, and the State Highway Patrolman ordered the first Negro who had beat to set on my feet to keep me from working my feet. I began to scream and one white man got up and began to beat me in my head and tell me to hush. One white man—my dress had worked up high, he walked over and pulled my dress down—and he pulled my dress back, back up.

*I was in jail when **Medgar Evers** was murdered.*

All of this is on account we want to register, to become first-class citizens, and if the Freedom Democratic Party is not seated now, I question America, is this America, the land of the free and the home of the brave where we have to sleep with our telephones off the hooks because our lives be threatened daily because we want to live as decent human beings, in America?

"Thank you." (Mills, pp. 119–21)

Medgar Evers: NAACP's Mississippi field secretary who was assassinated in 1963 at the age of thirty-seven.

What happened next...

The credentials committee, under tremendous pressure from the Johnson administration, refused to unseat the regular Mississippi Democrats. Instead, they offered the following compromise: the MFDP would be given two "at-large" seats in the convention (not representing the state of Mississippi); the Mississippi Democrats would have to swear loyalty to the party's presidential nominee before being seated; and in the future, only racially integrated delegations would be welcomed at the convention.

The majority of MFDP delegates rejected the compromise. "We didn't come all this way for no two seats when all of

us is tired," exclaimed Hamer. Nor were the regular Mississippi Democratic delegates happy with conditions imposed by the credentials committee. To demonstrate their displeasure they, along with the all-white delegation from Alabama, walked out of the convention.

The MFDP delegates accepted convention passes donated by delegates from other states and took seats on the convention floor. Hamer led the Mississippians in freedom songs before the group was removed by security officers.

Once the representatives returned home, the MFDP mounted campaigns of five candidates (one of whom was Hamer) for U.S. Congress. Since the regular Mississippi Democrats continued to exclude blacks from the primary, the Freedom Democrats staged their own elections. All five MFDP candidates received more votes than their "regular" Democratic opponents.

After the election an MFDP contingent traveled to Washington, D.C., to file an official protest against the Mississippi Democratic Party for its exclusion of blacks from the primary. After looking into the matter, Congress voted in favor of seating the regular Democrats. In protest, the MFDP sponsored a demonstration in front of the Capitol. "We'll come back year after year until we are allowed our rights as citizens," proclaimed Hamer.

The MFDP finally met with a measure of victory in 1968 at the Democratic national convention in Chicago. For that effort, MFDP activists joined with other liberal Mississippians to form a group called the Loyalist Democrats. The credentials committee, bound to uphold its promise of 1964, ousted the all-white regular Democratic Party delegates in favor of the racially mixed Loyalists. Hamer was among the Loyalist delegates to take a hard-earned seat at the convention.

Did you know...

- Hamer was left with permanent blurred vision and kidney damage as a result of the 1963 beating she suffered in the Winona jail.

- In 1965 *Mississippi* magazine named Hamer one of the state's six "women of influence." In the early 1970s the city of Ruleville began celebrating a Fannie Lou Hamer Day.

- For many seasoned civil rights activists, the failure of the national Democratic Party to recognize the MFDP at the 1964 convention was the ultimate betrayal by the liberal political establishment. Robert Moses spoke for many when he told television reporters: "I will have nothing to do with the political system any longer."

For More Information See

Books

Proceedings of the Democratic National Convention: 1964–Credentials Committee. Washington, D.C.: Democratic National Committee, 1964.

Sources

Books

African American Biography. Volume 2. Detroit: U•X•L, 1994, pp. 307–9.

Altman, Susan. *Encyclopedia of African-American Heritage.* New York: Facts on File, Inc., 1997, pp. 107–8.

Crawford, Vicki L., Jacqueline Anne Rouse, and Barbara Woods, eds. *Women in the Civil Rights Movement: Trailblazers and Torchbearers, 1941–1965.* Brooklyn, NY: Carlson Publishing, Inc., 1990.

Giddings, Paula. *When and Where I Enter: The Impact of Black Women on Race and Sex in America.* New York: Bantam Books, 1984.

Kling, Susan. *Fannie Lou Hamer: A Biography.* Chicago: Women for Racial and Economic Equality, 1979.

Lewis, John. *Walking with the Wind.* New York: Simon and Schuster, 1998.

Mills, Kay. *This Little Light of Mine: The Life of Fannie Lou Hamer.* New York: Dutton, 1993.

Williams, Juan. *Eyes on the Prize: America's Civil Rights Years, 1954–1965.* New York: Penguin Books, 1987.

Economic Rights

E conomic rights are the rights of individuals and groups of people (defined by race, ethnicity, gender, or other criteria) to a livelihood, to humane working conditions, and to fair wages. Economic rights are also be defined as the absence of exploitation or mistreatment in the workplace. During certain periods in the history of the United States (and in some cases, at present), various groups of people—such as Hispanic and Filipino farm workers, Native American fishers, women teachers, Asian American sweatshop employees, and Irish miners—have had their economic rights curtailed.

For farm workers, the majority of whom are of Mexican descent, a historical lack of economic rights has been well documented. Farm workers have suffered (and many still suffer) from exposure to dangerous pesticides, inadequate sanitation and housing facilities, and substandard wages.

The first large-scale campaign for the rights of farm workers occurred in the latter half of the 1960s. The United Farm Workers (UFW) union, under the direction of **César Chávez** (1927–1993), coordinated a strike by thousands of laborers in California's central San Joaquín Valley. The strike

Striking grape workers on the march. In March 1966 strikers embarked on a 250-mile-long "pilgrimage" from Delano, California, to the state capital of Sacramento. *Reproduced by permission of Corbis-Bettmann.*

lasted almost five years, ultimately securing for some 40,000 farm workers higher wages, protection from pesticides, and preferential hiring for union workers.

Filipino agricultural laborers have also faced a lack of economic rights in the agricultural fields. The best-known champion of Filipino workers' rights was **Philip Vera Cruz** (1904–1994). Vera Cruz came to the United States in 1926 and made his way to the agricultural fields and vineyards of the San Joaquín Valley in 1943. There he found Filipino farm workers receiving low wages, being mistreated by bosses, and living in squalid camps. Vera Cruz organized the Filipinos into a union, which later became part of the UFW.

Native Americans in the Northwest have been denied their right, guaranteed by treaty, to fish without infringement by state or local laws. From the late 1800s through the mid-1970s, police and game wardens tried to prohibit traditional Native American fishing practices. In so doing, they denied

Native Americans from engaging in the vocation that had sustained their people for centuries.

The Survival of American Indians Association, Inc.—a group of mostly Nisqually, Tulalip, and Puyallup Indians whose livelihoods depended on fishing in the Nisqually and Quillayute Rivers—led the fight to defend Native American fishing rights. Among the group's founders was Janet McCloud, whose daughter, **Laura McCloud**, recorded the events of one fishing rights demonstration and the subsequent trial of the people arrested at the demonstration. In 1974 Judge George H. Boldt (1903–) of the federal court for the District of Washington State upheld the rights of Native Americans to fish without state interference in the landmark court case *United States v. Washington.*

César Chávez

"Where Harassment Backfires"

**Excerpt from *César Chávez: Autobiography of La Causa*
Published in 1975**

More than three million Mexican agricultural workers came to the United States during the 1950s and 1960s. They traded the poverty and unemployment of their homeland for the back-breaking work, exposure to dangerous pesticides, and meager wages of American fields and vineyards. Many of the laborers migrated up and down central California's San Joaquín Valley, working their way from one grape harvest to the next.

In the early 1960s most farm workers earned less than $2,000 per year—barely enough to survive on. In many cases, the wages a farm worker earned were significantly less than what they had been promised by the grower. Since most farm workers did not speak English, had no political or economic power base in the United States, and lived in constant fear of deportation, they were unable to fight back against growers' injustices.

Most farm workers lived in rundown one-room shacks with no heat or running water. Those who had no money for housing slept under their vehicles. The average life expectancy of a farm worker in 1965 was forty-nine years; by contrast, the average life expectancy of a white U.S. citizen was seventy years.

We mean to have our peace, and to win it without violence, for it is violence we would overcome—the subtle and spiritual violence of oppression.

The Delano Grape Workers' Boycott Day Proclamation

On February 14, 1968, César Chávez began a fast in support of the farm workers' strike. At the end of his fast—which lasted twenty-five days—Chávez broke bread with Senator Robert F. Kennedy.
Reproduced by permission of Corbis-Bettmann.

In 1962 César Chávez (1927–1993) and two other organizers—Dolores Huerta (1930–) and Gilberto Padillo—headed into the fields around Delano, California, and began talking with farm workers about ways to improve their working conditions. Within three years, the organizers had enlisted 1,700 members in their group, the National Farm Workers Association (NFWA).

In September 1965 the NFWA was approached by the Agricultural Workers Organizing Committee (AWOC)—a union of Filipino farm workers—which asked for support. The 600 members of AWOC had gone on strike, and the growers had responded by firing the strikers and throwing them out of their homes. The AWOC requested that the NFWA join them in the strike.

On September 16, 1965 (Mexican Independence Day), the Mexican farm workers voted to go on strike. The workers took this action even though it meant risking their jobs and possibly facing deportation. The next day, NFWA workers walked out of the vineyards surrounding Delano. They demanded a living wage, decent housing, and humane working conditions. By the end of the strike's first week, 3,000 farm workers had left their jobs on dozens of farms in the San Joaquín Valley. In the following excerpt, Chávez describes the early days of the strike.

Things to remember while reading "Where Harassment Backfires":

- One way in which the growers responded to the strike was by hiring scabs (people brought in to work by employers when employees go on strike; called "replacement workers" by growers) to take the place of the strikers in the fields. The strikers tried to talk the scabs out of working and into joining them on the picket lines.

- The growers also opposed the strike by obtaining injunctions—legal documents that prohibited workers from picketing on or near the growers' property. Through a series of injunctions, growers were able to keep workers from picketing in fields, along roadsides, and in front of growers' homes. The injunctions forced the farm workers to adopt other strategies, most notably the grape boycott.

- César Chávez advocated nonviolence—the rejection of all forms of violence. He argued that a lasting moral victory could only be achieved through nonviolent means. In February 1968 some union members, frustrated by the long strike, spoke of committing acts of sabotage against crops and equipment. Chávez's response was to demonstrate the power of nonviolent action by undertaking a twenty-five-day fast.

"Where Harassment Backfires"

We were up before dawn Monday morning. Before the day was over, more than twelve hundred workers had joined the strike in an area covering about four hundred square miles of vineyards.

There was a lot of excitement, a lot of optimism, and a tremendous amount of activity. In those days we didn't know how to organize the people for maximum production, and there was a lot of wasted effort, a lot of people constantly coming and going.

Our office was a little store at the corner of First and Albany, no bigger than 20 by 40 feet, and it was jam-packed. We used it as an office, as a service center, as a dormitory, and as a meeting hall. We never closed. And we were picketing every day, getting up very early each morning and going to bed very late at night.

Ironically, although in the Mexican custom the man is really the boss of the house, once the strike started, women became freer quicker than the men. And it's been our experience everywhere since then. The women are not afraid. They know what they're doing because it means beans and shoes for their kids.

Sometimes pickets asked, "What's the use of picketing?" because they were picketing and couldn't even see the people working deep in the vineyards. The answer was that they affected production.

*"Just keep talking to the **scabs**," I said. "After a while, if it's done the right way, they begin to leave. Somebody else may take their place, or it looks like the job is filled, but it isn't really. There's a loss of time. The grower is getting people who are not experienced, who have never seen grapes in their lives. For the employer that's loss of money."*

"We've got to make the grower spend fifty dollars to our one dollar," I said. "We affect production and costs and profit. And if we hold out, we can win."

In addition, to me the picket line is something very special. Unless you have been on a picket line, you just can't understand the feeling you get there, seeing the conflict at its two most acid ends. It's a confrontation that's vivid. It's a real education.

Without knowing it, the workers also had more than just a picket line; they had the nerve to be in a picket line and to be striking.

The growers were very angry at the challenge. How dare they strike the bosses! Both surprised and hurt, they struck back. On the first day, I left two workers to picket the entrance of a ranch near the office. A short time later they were back, breathless.

"What happened?" I asked. "Where's your car?" They had run about a mile to the office.

Scabs: Workers hired to take the place of, and weaken the resolve of, striking workers.

They said a grower had pointed a shotgun at them and threatened to kill them. He grabbed their picket signs, set them on fire, and when they didn't burn fast enough, he blasted the signs with his shotgun.

The incident was reported to the police, but nothing happened.

A few days later, when we had about six or seven pickets in front of a labor contractor's home, about twenty or thirty growers came over there half-drunk from a party. Julio Hernandez ran to tell me that the growers had beaten one of our men. So I went over and got on the picket line.

The growers were giving us the knee and the elbow, knocking us down and throwing us down. But we remained nonviolent. We weren't afraid of them. We just got up and continued picketing.

A big crowd started forming, booing the growers. Then the Filipinos, who were having a meeting in Filipino Hall, got in their cars and raced over. The growers suddenly were surrounded by angry people. Police, sheriff's deputies, and the fire department arrived.

One of the growers started getting rough with one of the cops, who put him in his patrol car, handcuffed him, and drove him to jail. There they released him. When we finally left, we were bruised, and I had sore ribs and legs and back for a while. Nothing happened to the growers.

As days passed, there was more violence. Growers pushed people around on the picket lines, ran tractors between pickets and the field to cover them with dust and dirt, and drove cars and pickups with guns and dogs dangerously close to pickets at high speeds.

One day, when Episcopal Bishop Sumner Walters joined our pickets, he was a victim of one of those dust attacks. Later, one grower used his sulphur rig to spray the pickets. When he finally was tried, he was acquitted.

Another time **Dolores** was coming back from a picket line with other people, and their car began to boil over. When they stopped by a house to get water, a grower came charging out of the house with a shotgun, which he fired over their heads.

During the first days of the strike things looked very good—as they usually do—then about the sixth day, did they look bad. From then on it was a seesaw battle.

There were days when we got all kinds of strikebreakers out of the fields. On others we didn't. At times they'd almost drive us out, and we'd regroup our strength and come back again. Sometimes we couldn't even go picketing because there were so many **injunctions**.

Dolores Huerta: 1930– ; cofounder of the United Farm Workers.

Injunctions: Legal documents requiring certain persons to refrain from a particular activity.

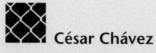

César Chávez

César Chávez was born on March 31, 1927, in Yuma, Arizona, to a poor farming family. The family lost its farm during the Great Depression (the worst economic crisis ever to hit the United States, lasting from 1929 to 1939). At the age of ten, Chávez and the rest of his family became migrant farm workers. They harvested crops throughout Arizona and California.

In 1952 Chávez moved to Delano, California, and went to work for the Community Service Organization (CSO). The CSO was a civil rights organization that helped people of Mexican heritage gain U.S. citizenship and register to vote. Chávez left the CSO ten years later in order to devote his energies to organizing farm workers. Chávez convinced two other CSO staffers to join him in establishing the National Farm Workers Association (NFWA), which later changed its name to the United Farm Workers (UFW).

César Chávez. *Reproduced by permission of Corbis-Bettmann.*

In 1965 Chávez's farm workers' union began its historic strike against California grape growers, which ended in victory in 1970. Chávez, who died in 1993 while on UFW business, is widely considered to have been the greatest Mexican American civil rights leader in history.

We could hardly move. Other times we weren't picketing because we didn't have any gas for the cars—we didn't have any money at all. Our guys went for about six months without getting a bill paid for anything. And we were discouraged.

More than once the authorities threatened to close our office down. Some of the people that were sent to do a job on us obviously didn't like it at all. I don't remember who it was, but I think it was the fire marshall who hated the politics of his assignment and told us so on more than one occasion. But they kept up their investigations under the health and building codes and the fire code. They were just on the verge of knocking us completely out, but we lucked out.

There was constant intimidation and harassment. Every single person who came to our office had his license plate number taken down. If he went to town, he would be stopped and questioned.

Of course, after a while, we welcomed this because every time the cops stopped these people, they'd get madder and help us more.

Those early days were really mean. We had cops stationed at our office and our homes around the clock. Every time I got in the car in Delano, they'd follow me all over, and I wouldn't shake them until I was well past several towns. Then they'd leave me and go back.

One of the first jobs we had to do was to get our people conditioned, so they wouldn't be afraid of the police. If they're not afraid, then they can keep a lot of things cool, but the moment they're uncertain, then anything can happen.

There was other harassment on the picket lines. At one point, after we had been on strike for about five or six weeks, we were stopped constantly by deputies. Every striker was photographed, and a field-report card was filled in on each person. In some cases, it took as much as an hour and a half to go through this process. Then it was repeated every time we moved from one field to another. We have a man in Delano who was photographed, and the same report was filled in on him no less than twelve times.

At first our tactic was total cooperation. Then we started taking their time. In my case, the officer took almost an hour because I went very slowly. I examined the card and the spelling, and I engaged in conversation just to tie him up.

Then we'd go on night picketing, get about thirty cars and go out at night, and they'd have to wake up the cops to follow us. We worked it so they had to have three shifts. If we'd go out of the office at 3:00 in the morning, they'd follow us.

With us, it was a tactic to get them to spend as much money as possible. The county spent thousands of dollars on extra personnel. They'll never spend that much money again. Afterward there were a lot of complaints. A small group of liberals in Bakersfield checked up on the expense and found they had spent thousands of dollars.

Proclamation of the Delano Grape Workers for International Boycott Day, May 10, 1969

In early 1969 striking farm workers intensified the grape boycott. United Farm Worker (UFW) organizers fanned out across the United States to coordinate local boycott efforts. Within one year, UFW supporters had convinced supermarket chains in Detroit, New York City (where grape sales fell by 95 percent), and several other large cities to stop carrying nonunion grapes.

The UFW proclaimed May 10, 1969, to be International Boycott Day. The group issued its proclamation that same day. It was originally published in the April 15-30, 1969, edition of *El Malcriado*. In part, the proclamation read:

> *We, the striking grape workers of California, join on this International Boycott Day with the consumers across the continent in planning the steps that lie ahead on the road to our liberation. As we plan, we recall the footsteps that brought us to this day and the events of this day. The historic road of our pilgrimage to Sacramento later branched out, spreading like the unpruned vines in struck fields, until it led us to willing exile in cities across this land. There, far from the earth we tilled for generations, we have cultivated the strange soil of public understanding....*
>
> *We have been farm workers for hundreds of years and pioneers for seven. Mexicans, Filipinos, Africans and others, our ancestors were among those who founded this land and tamed its natural wilderness.... We are conscious today of the significance of our present quest. If this road we chart leads to the rights and reforms we demand ... then in our wake will follow thousands of American farm workers. Our example will make them free....*
>
> *We have been farm workers for hundreds of years and strikers for four. It*

Finally we made up our minds we had been harassed enough. We refused to give them any information or to let them take our pictures. We told the inquiring officer from the Kern County Sheriff's Office that if he wanted more information from us or wanted to take our picture, he would first have to arrest us. And at that point we were able to gain some ground. (Levy, pp. 187–90)

What happened next...

Farm workers, stymied by injunctions against picketing, were forced to employ other strategies in the strike. One was four years ago that we threw down our plowshares and pruning hooks. These Biblical symbols of peace and tranquility to us represent too many lifetimes of unprotesting submission to a degrading social system that allows us no dignity, no comfort, no peace. We mean to have our peace, and to win it without violence, for it is violence we would overcome.... So we went and stood tall outside the vineyards where we had stooped for years. But the tailors of national labor legislation had left us naked.... [O]ur picket lines were crippled by injunctions and harassed by growers; our strike was broken by imported scabs; our overtures to our employers were ignored. Yet we knew the day must come when they would talk to us, as equals.

We have been farm workers for hundreds of years and boycotters for two. We did not choose the grape boycott, but we had chosen to leave our peonage, poverty and despair behind.... The boycott was the only way forward the growers left to us. We called upon our fellow men and were answered by consumers who said—as all men of conscience must—that they would no longer allow their tables to be subsidized by our sweat and our sorrow....

We marched alone at the beginning, but today we count men of all creeds, nationalities, and occupations in our number. Between us and the justice we seek now stand the large and powerful grocers who, in continuing to buy table grapes, betray the boycott their own customers have built. These stores treat their patrons' demands to remove the grapes the same way the growers treat our demands for union recognition—by ignoring them....

Grapes must remain an unenjoyed luxury for all as long as the barest human needs and basic human rights are still luxuries for farm workers. The grapes grow sweet and heavy on the vines, but they will have to wait while we reach out first for our freedom. The time is ripe for our liberation.

of the union's earliest and most effective initiatives was a boycott of California table grapes. The farm workers appealed to American citizens to stop buying grapes as a way of putting economic pressure on the growers. Students, religious leaders, labor unions, and civil rights organizations from throughout the nation rallied to the farm workers' cause. They promoted the boycott in their communities and persuaded grocers not to carry grapes.

In March 1966, as the strike entered its sixth month, the strikers embarked on a 250-mile-long "pilgrimage" (so-called because of its religious overtones; most of the farm workers were Catholic) from Delano to the state capital of Sacramento. The purpose of the pilgrimage was to renew the commitment of striking workers, to make contact with farm workers outside of Delano, and to refocus national attention on the struggle. Twenty-one days into the march, the strikers received word that one of the largest grape growers, the Schenley Corporation, had given in to the strikers' demands. The agreement with Schenley was the first major farm labor contract in U.S. history.

Following that settlement, the NFWA and the AWOC merged to form the United Farm Workers (UFW) and joined with the nation's largest labor conglomerate, the AFL-CIO (American Federation of Labor-Congress of Industrial Organizations). The UFW next set its sights on winning concessions from the remaining growers.

On July 29, 1970, nearly five years after the strike had begun and after growers had sustained significant financial losses due to the grape boycott, the twenty-six remaining Delano grape growers finally yielded to workers' demands. The contracts guaranteed the 40,000 farm workers represented by the UFW the following: $1.80 per hour plus 20 cents per box of grapes picked; protection against pesticides; seniority for striking workers; and a union hiring hall.

Did you know...

- In 1984 the UFW renewed the call for a boycott of all California table grapes not bearing the UFW label (the only brand exempted from the boycott is Nash de Camp's Sun Power). The primary reason for the boycott, which is still in place, is the growers' application of dangerous pesticides to the grapes—even to "organic" grapes. Some of these pesticides have been shown to cause cancer and birth defects.

- In September 1998 the U.S. Department of Labor uncovered safety and minimum-wage violations in 77 percent of the California grape vineyards inspected. Violations included the underpayment of workers, the hiring of underage workers, and the provision of unsafe housing and transportation for workers.

Sources

Books

Cedeño, Maria E. *César Chávez: Labor Leader*. Brookfield, CT: Millbrook Press, 1993.

Cockroft, James D. *The Hispanic Struggle for Social Justice*. New York: Franklin Watts, 1994.

Ferriss, Susan, and Ricardo Sandoval. *The Fight in the Fields: César Chávez and the Farmworkers Movement*. New York: Harcourt Brace and Company, 1997.

Griswold del Castillo, Richard, and Richard A. Garcia. *César Chávez: A Triumph of Sprit*. Norman, Oklahoma: University of Oklahoma Press, 1995.

Levy, Jacques. *César Chávez: Autobiography of La Causa*. New York: W. W. Norton, 1975.

Martinez, Elizabeth Sutherland, and Enriqueta Longeaux y Vásquez. *Viva la Raza!: The Struggle of the Mexican-American People*. Garden City, NY: Doubleday and Company, Inc., 1974.

Nagel, Rob, and Sharon Rose, eds. *Hispanic American Biography*. Vols. 1 and 2. Detroit: U•X•L, 1995, pp. 41–45 (vol. 1); pp. 223–25 (vol. 2).

Rosales, F. Arturo. *Chicano! The History of the Mexican American Civil Rights Movement*. Houston, TX: Arte Público Press, 1997.

Steiner, Stan. *La Raza: The Mexican-Americans*. New York: Harper and Row, 1969.

Periodicals

"Probe of State Vineyards Finds Labor Violations." *Los Angeles Times*. September 16, 1998: A-24.

Web Sites

United Farm Workers. [Online] Available http://www.ufw.org/ (last accessed on March 23, 1999).

Other

Chicano! The History of the Mexican American Civil Rights Movement (videocassette; four episodes). Los Angeles: NLCC Educational Media, 1996.

Philip Vera Cruz

"Sour Grapes: Symbol of Oppression"
Excerpt from *Roots: An Asian American Reader*
Published in 1971

Filipino agricultural laborers first came to California in the latter half of the 1920s, to work on citrus and vegetable farms. Similar to the situation confronting Chinese and Japanese workers, Filipinos were welcomed by employers for their cheap labor. At the same time, they were shunned by non-Asian workers who saw them as unwanted competition.

The Great Depression was an especially difficult time for the 45,000 Filipinos in the continental United States. (The Great Depression was the worst economic crisis ever to hit the United States, lasting from 1929 through 1939.) White vigilante groups conducted violent raids on Filipino worker camps, and nativist organizations lobbied Congress to deport the Filipinos. (The type of behavior in which the dominant group blames its economic woes on "outsiders" and demands their expulsion is called nativism.) Filipino workers responded to the oppression by forming labor unions, often with other racial minorities, to defend their rights.

Filipino labor leader Philip Vera Cruz (1904–1994) migrated to the United States in 1926 at the age of twenty-two. He expected to find a well-paying job so he could save money,

"Conscience and justice are foreign to the ruthless nature of agribusiness. Equipped with the right to property, agribusiness is turning the United States into a fascist state."

Filipino grape workers in central California. Philip Vera Cruz was appalled by the low wages workers received, the mistreatment of workers by managers, and the terrible conditions of the worker camps. *Reproduced by permission of UPI/Corbis-Bettmann.*

put himself through school, and support his family in the Philippines. Instead, Vera Cruz found low-paying employment and racial discrimination.

After working for several years in the canneries of Alaska and restaurants in Chicago, Vera Cruz, in 1943, made his way to the agricultural fields and vineyards of central California's San Joaquín Valley. There Vera Cruz witnessed the poverty of the field workers, and the multi-billion-dollar per year agricultural industry those workers supported. Vera Cruz was appalled by the low wages workers received, the mistreatment of workers by managers, and the terrible conditions of the worker camps.

Vera Cruz also took note of discrimination against Filipino workers in the towns. Like other people of color, Filipinos were made to sit in segregated sections of movie theaters. They were treated rudely by grocery store owners and restaurant proprietors and brutalized by the police.

In the early 1960s Vera Cruz participated in the formation of the mostly Filipino Agricultural Workers Organizing Committee (AWOC). After a series of small strikes throughout the San Joaquín Valley, 600 AWOC members went on strike in the grape fields of Coachella on September 8, 1965. The growers responded by firing the workers and throwing them out of the camps.

The Filipino workers then turned to the mostly Mexican National Farm Workers Association (NFWA)—led by César Chávez (1927–1993)—for support in nearby Delano. On September 16, NFWA members voted to join the strike.

Six months after that, the two unions merged to form the United Farm Workers (UFW). César Chávez became president of the UFW, and Vera Cruz was named a vice president. On July 29, 1970, nearly five years after the strike had begun, it ended in victory. Grape growers signed contracts guaranteeing higher wages and better working conditions for 40,000 agricultural workers.

Things to remember while reading "Sour Grapes: Symbol of Oppression":

- Like so many other Filipinos (and immigrants of other nationalities), Vera Cruz experienced disillusionment and disappointment after his arrival in the United States. "All the stories we heard were only success stories," stated Vera Cruz in his 1992 biography entitled *Philip Vera Cruz: A Personal History of Filipino Immigrants and the Farmworkers Movement.* "So my plan was to finish college in America, get a good job over there, save my money, and then return home and support my family. It was only after I finally got to America that I understood how different reality was for us Filipinos."

- Filipinos, like other Asian Americans, Hispanic Americans, Native Americans, and other people of color in the southwestern United States, were prohibited from using the same public and private facilities as whites. Segregation—the separation of the races, as dictated by laws and social customs—was best known as the social system used against African Americans in the South from the 1890s through the

1960s. The purpose of segregation was to relegate certain races of people to the status of second-class citizens.

"Sour Grapes: Symbol of Oppression"

From the slum district in the near Northside across the river in Chicago, I came and lived in the shantytowns in California. Being used to city life, I thought I would go back and be with my friends again. Instead I started working in the grape vineyards in the early Spring of 1943 and stayed on until the Delano Grape Strike in September 1965.

For the first few years in California, I considered Delano as my hometown. Though I went to work in the Arvin-Lamont area for thinning plums, picking and packing grapes for different growers, cut raisin grapes in Selma, cut asparagus in Byron and worked in the salmon cannery in Alaska, I always returned to Delano. There was nothing especially interesting for me about the old town. But, as I was a stranger in the state, it was the only place where I met most of my new friends.

While in town on Saturdays, I would walk across the railroad tracks to the business district comprising about two and a half blocks between the 9th and 12th avenues in Main Street. Country people coming to town once a week lined up the sidewalks and flocked into those few stores. Parents brought their children with them for new experiences in life.

There was a bank, a post office and a theater. All were small but quaint. Employees like those in the stores were lily-white, arrogant and sarcastic. You could always feel their sense of racial superiority.

The Delano Theater practiced racial segregation.

Seats in the northside and in the center were reserved for whites only. A small part of the theater in the southside was for the minority grape-pickers—Orientals, Mexicans, Blacks, Puerto Ricans, Arabs, etc. People didn't like or care for each other but themselves.

Even the attitude of the Filipinos towards their own people was cold with indifference. An unpleasant thrill runs through my spine by

Segregation: The separation of the races, as dictated by laws and social customs.

just looking at acquaintances as they pass me by without the slightest sign of a friendly greeting. I had talked to them before and even ate with them at the same tables, but they moved around me as if we never met. This prevalent attitude has been hurting people. Communication among them was very slight because of strained personal relations. But, this damaging attitude is just a faint reflection of a racist community.

Filipinos in Delano have worked in the grape vineyards for a long time. Some of them told me the common practice of hiring during the depression years. They said that "in the pruning season, a grower required new employees to get to the labor camp two of three days, or more, for training without pay. In the training and practice period, those new helps were charged 75 cents for board a day. At least the black slaves in the South had their meals free." But, those Filipino trainees paid theirs while working in an **agribusiness** ranch for gratis. Then, after those recruits learned the job, they were paid ten to fifteen cents an hour.

Filipino farm workers at the dedication of the Agbayani Village retirement center in 1974. Philip Vera Cruz and César Chávez pioneered the construction of the center, which provides low-rent housing for elderly farm workers. *Photograph by Bob Fitch. Reproduced by permission of AP/Wide World Photos.*

Agribusiness: Farming businesses operated as a large-scale industry.

In those depression years, Filipinos were blamed for taking the Anglos' jobs. Racist growers and politicians picked on the Filipino minority as an easy target for discrimination and attack. Filipinos were harassed and driven from their camps. But, the sad thing was they didn't have anywhere else to go. They were pushed to the wall and the whole town was against them. The police made false arrests and threw them in jail. In certain cases the courts imposed excessive fines. Those poor unwanted people risked their lives even just to go and buy their groceries. In those race riots staged in their camps, some were hurt and one was shot dead in bed.

While working in different labor camps in the Delano area, I observed that on Saturdays and Sundays during the harvest grape seasons, Filipinos concentrated in Chinatown west of the railroad tracks. (The habit still continued to the present.) They were not welcome in other places in town, so they didn't have any other place to go. Though their job was strenuous, it was also monotonous. After the day's work was done, a quick shower and hurried dinner, they would walk slowly by a small restaurant, or bar, and go close to those windows, screen their eyes and peep through to see who was there. They seemed to be always looking for someone, or some acquaintances or friends, but really there were no particular people in their minds.

There were many standing in groups talking about grapes—names of growers, location of ranches, acreage, wages and bonuses, hours of work, cooks, board per day, etc. Most important was how the growers were. Were they reasonable to work for? To go through that noisy crowd, one had to take a detour or get off from the sidewalk to the middle of Glenwood Street.

The whole sidewalk in Chinatown was the busiest Employment Service in all Delano. It was an open HIRING HALL for the Filipino grape pickers. A foreman or anyone ordered to get an additional worker by a grower was a dispatcher. One could be hired in Chinatown but rejected when reporting on the job, or one could be accepted and later fired without reasons. That was why even a small owner acted like a dictator. Right or wrong, or wise or foolish, his word was law. He was the supreme court whose decision was absolute.

Other Filipino brothers were quite shy. Some of them were just standing and watching the passers-by, or looking at the north end of that buzzing sidewalk then turning to the south to see what was happening. There were some squatting or sitting on copies of the DELANO RECORD on the edge of the sidewalk. Like brown owls, they *turned their head from one side to the other to check if the entire flock along the block was still in peace.*

Moving into the restaurants, bars, cardrooms and pool halls, I sometimes found them packed with Filipino grapepickers. For a change of environment on weekends, they didn't mind paying the high prices on the menu or for beer at the bar. Some were hungry and eating, others were just lingering around and flirting with the waitresses or girls behind the bar. Cardrooms and pool halls were usually together. Women were all over the place participating in all those activities. The whole business looked like a mixed-up affair.

One might prefer to go to the pool hall. To feel and look important, he would walk erectly, seemingly with dignity, stop at the counter and survey those Havana cigars, and would fill his shirt pocket with those long fat cigars. Lighting and smoking a big cigar in the corner of his mouth gave him the feeling and semblance of a prosperous grower, or maybe a banker. But, he could be easing his nervousness or could just be addicted to that habit-forming stimulant.

In that pool hall, sputum of tobacco juice spotted the floor along the walls, especially in the corners. Reflected against the bright light, the gamblers in the adjoining room played cards or dominos in the cloud of smoke. After inhaling that foul air for several years, each made his saddest and loneliest first, and maybe his last trip—to the tuberculosis sanitarium. Loss of precious health and lives were the unnecessary but inevitably cruel effect of forced racial segregation.

Sometimes a squabble would start in a cardroom. A guy got caught cheating in a "paralasi game" and another stood up and pulled a knife on him. The others grabbed the former to calm him down, while the latter ran quickly out through the door knocking down a few men sitting and talking on the sidewalk.

Another fight ensued, worse than the first one. At this time, more men were involved. Thinking that those fights and the confusion were giving the business a bad reputation, the proprietor called the Delano Police Department. He believed that the good relations he had with the city police would always help him with his headaches with those roughnecks.

Within a few minutes, the police arrived and mixed with the crowd. Not knowing who were fighting, they arrested people on the sidewalk at random. But, before the police left, the chief gave a stern, curt statement, "You are supposed to be in the labor camps to pick grapes when the growers need you. If you don't do that, then go back

Philip Vera Cruz

Philip Vera Cruz (1904–1994) was born in Ilocos Sur, the Philippines, on December 25, 1904. He came to the United States in search of work in 1926, with the hope of saving money and supporting his family in the Philippines. Between 1926 and 1942 Vera Cruz worked at a series of low-paying, menial jobs in canneries, restaurants, agricultural fields, and hotels. In 1943 he moved to Delano, California, in the San Joaquín Valley, and began working in the grape vineyards.

Appalled at the low pay and horrible working conditions of agricultural work, Vera Cruz began organizing the farm workers to stand up for their rights. Together with Mexican American labor leader César Chávez (1927–1993) and other organizers, Vera Cruz was instrumental in the founding of the United Farm Workers (UFW) union.

Vera Cruz served as a vice president of the UFW from 1966 to 1977. In that position Vera Cruz promoted coalition-building across racial lines and stressed the importance of participatory democracy—a system in which every union member has a role in shaping the organization. He continued to be active in the labor movement and various social justice issues until his death in 1994.

where you belong, or I'll throw you all in jail. I don't want to see you here in town again."

An elderly man, reflecting on what had happened that evening remarked, "All these people have been moving from one place to the other. Wherever I went, there was a place for Filipinos to gather together and just be among themselves. Like any other **rendezvous** of our people (a slum district), Chinatown in Delano is a hobos' paradise. Unfortunately, most Filipino community leaders have taken advantage of this situation. They choose to live on the rackets—bars for the disgusted and despondent, gambling for the unjust and greedy, and dance halls for the lonely and unhappy. These businesses are the sources of easy but questionable money. But, since they are at the mercy of the city council, police and sheriff department, the proprietors align themselves with them and exploit the minorities. They must make money to stay in the rackets. They would sell a guy for a few dollars because they themselves have no guiding principles." As

Rendezvous: Meeting place.

*the growers control the town, so do these leaders take the employers'
side in a labor dispute with management.*

*The next morning, the people in Chinatown went to work for the
first picking of the seedless Thompson grapes. With many years of
experience, they know grapes. They complained that the bunches
were too green. But the growers gave the orders, through their ranch
managers and foremen, to pick and pack more for the "high prices in
the market." The workers were bothered with their conscience but
could not use their own judgement. So, they worked as ordered.*

*In the afternoon, an inspector went to a packing house and
tested the packed grapes. He found the content deficient and told the
owners to stop the picking.*

*The whole crew was ordered to repack the green grapes, without
pay. While all the workers were busy repacking, the inspector was
closely watching them. But when he went away, the big grower himself was there and told them to load those sour grapes, first into the
boxcar with the repacked boxes on top. This is one of the magic tricks
of the growers in the table-grape industry.*

*With brands from other ranches, the Delano Sour Grapes were
sent as delicacies to the metropolis of the United States. The uniform
bunches and solid berries, packed beautifully, could have been the
choice grapes of the world if the growers had waited just a few more
days for Nature to sweeten the fruit.*

*Premature harvest in the grape industry has been the common
practice of the family farm and agribusiness. It is caused by cut-throat
competition tainted with deceit and unsatisfied personal greed. Customers spend their money for sour grapes not fit to eat. The orders
from the growers overpower the conscience and decency of workers to
do what is right in their work.*

*Those accumulated profits of agribusiness are generating eco-
nomic power for the oppression and enslavement of farm workers.
They are used to influence legislation to enhance agribusiness interests in an ever expanding growth. They perpetuate poverty and shantytowns located in the richest states of the nation. For the children,
living in those filthy shacks is a disaster to their welfare and future.
Conscience and justice are foreign to the ruthless nature of agribusiness. Equipped with the right to property, agribusiness is turning the
United States into a* **fascist** *state. Excessive expansion and oppressive
power of agribusiness must be checked as a protection for the people's
rights. (Tachiki, et al, pp. 302–04)*

Fascist: A political philosophy
that places nation and race
above the individual. Fascist
governments are run by a
single, dictatorial leader and
are characterized by extreme
social and economic
restrictions.

What happened next...

Vera Cruz remained a vice president of the UFW, and one of the union's most effective organizers, until his resignation in 1977. Vera Cruz stepped down from the UFW because of a longstanding rift between himself and César Chávez. Vera Cruz, who felt the union should take its direction from the membership, disagreed with the hierarchical leadership structure of the UFW. He was particularly dismayed by the cult of personality that had formed around Chávez, the charismatic leader at the helm of the union.

Vera Cruz was also opposed to the UFW's policy of only supporting farm workers who were in the United States with the proper immigration documentation. Vera Cruz stressed the importance of standing up for the human rights of all people—even "illegal" workers.

The final straw for Vera Cruz was Chávez's support for Filipino dictator Ferdinand Marcos (Marcos ruled the Philippines from 1965 to 1986). While Vera Cruz adamantly opposed the corrupt and authoritarian Marcos regime, Chávez accepted a Presidential Appreciation Award from Marcos in 1977.

Did you know...

- By sending home portions of his meager earnings over the years, Vera Cruz was able to finance the college educations of his younger siblings and their children in the Philippines.

- In 1987 Corazon Aquino, the new, democratically elected president of the Philippines, presented Vera Cruz with an award for lifelong service to the Filipino community in the United States.

For More Information See

Periodicals

Girda (Asian American newsmonthly from Los Angeles). November 1970.

Sources

Books

Chan, Sucheng. *Asian Americans: An Interpretive History.* Boston: Twayne Publishers, 1991.

Cordova, Fred. *Filipinos, Forgotten Asian Americans: A Pictorial History.* Dubuque, IA: Kendall/Hunt Publishing Company, 1983.

Crouchett, Lorraine Jacobs. *Filipinos in California: From the Days of the Galleons to the Present.* El Cerrito, CA: Downey Place Publishing House, 1982.

Karnow, Stanley. *In Our Image: America's Empire in the Philippines.* New York: Foreign Policy Association, 1989.

Scharlin, Craig, and Lilia V. Villanueva. *Philip Vera Cruz: A Personal History of Filipino Immigrants and the Farmworkers Movement.* Los Angeles: UCLA Labor Center, 1992.

Sinnott, Susan. *Extraordinary Asian Pacific Americans.* Chicago: Children's Press, 1993, pp. 70–72.

Tachiki, Amy, et al, eds. *Roots: An Asian American Reader.* Los Angeles: UCLA Asian American Studies Center, 1971.

Periodicals

Lyons, Richard D. "Philip Vera Cruz, 89; Helped to Found Farm Worker Union" (obituary). *New York Times.* June 16, 1994: B9.

Laura McCloud

"The New Indian Wars"

**Excerpt from *Native American Testimony: A Chronicle of Indian-White Relations from Prophecy to the Present, 1492–1992*
Published in 1991**

B eginning in the late 1800s, lawmakers in Washington state attempted to ban traditional Native American fishing practices. Law enforcement officials began arresting Indians who were fishing with nets or fishing at times outside of the established "fishing season." The officials, however, were acting in violation of treaties, signed in the 1850s, that exempted Native Americans from state-imposed fishing restrictions.

State lawmakers claimed they were trying to protect the dwindling salmon supply in the rivers that ran inland from Puget Sound; they blamed the salmon reduction on over-fishing by Indians. Native Americans responded that the salmon loss was not caused by their traditional fishing but by pollution of the river, the construction of dams, and commercial fishing operations—all at the hands of non-Indians.

In the mid-1960s tensions over Indian fishing rights in Washington's Puget Sound area came to a head. Game wardens and other law enforcement officials attempted to stop Indians from fishing by beating and arresting them, ramming their fishing boats, and cutting their nets.

"So the war goes on—which goes to prove that the history books are wrong when they talk about 'the last Indian wars.' They have never stopped!"

A Native American fishing rights demonstration in Olympia, Washington, on February 19, 1966.
Reproduced by permission of AP/Wide World Photos.

Native Americans organized a resistance to these tactics. Leading the charge was The Survival of American Indians Association, Inc.—a group of mostly Nisqually, Tulalip, and Puyallup Indians whose livelihoods depended on fishing in the Nisqually and Quillayute Rivers. They were supported by the National Indian Youth Council—a group of young, mostly urban Indian activists from Albuquerque, New Mexico—and Chicanos from the Seattle organization El Centro de la Raza.

Beginning in 1964, activists held several "fish-ins" in northwestern Washington state. (A fish-in is a protest in which activists purposely violate state fishing laws, in order to assert their treaty rights.) Hundreds of Indian activists were arrested during fish-ins; many were beaten by clubwielding police and game wardens. Some were shot at by white vigilante (citizens who take criminal justice matters into their own hands) sports fishermen. The Indians garnered national attention when actors Marlon Brando, Jane Fonda, and Dick Gregory joined the demonstrations.

Janet McCloud (1935–), a Tulalip/Nisqually Indian and a mother of eight, was a founding member of The Survival of American Indians Association, Inc. McCloud became well known among Native Americans in the 1960s and 1970s for her courage and her commitment to safeguarding Indian treaty rights. McCloud was one of six Indians arrested during a fish-in on the Nisqually River on October 13, 1965 (another of the six was McCloud's husband, a Puyallup Indian). In the following report, McCloud's daughter, Laura, describes the fish-in arrests and the activists' trial, held three years later.

Things to remember while reading "The New Indian Wars":

- The fish-ins were the first civil disobedience campaign of the American Indian rights movement (also called the "Red Power" movement) of the 1960s and 1970s. Civil disobedience is a form of nonviolent action in which participants refuse to obey certain laws, with the purpose of challenging the fairness of those laws. The fish-ins were inspired by the sit-ins of the African American civil rights movement, in which black students demanded service at "whites-only" lunch counters and bus terminals throughout the South in the early 1960s.

- As Laura McCloud recounts, the fishing-rights activists doubted that they would receive a fair trial. Their fear was well founded. The Indian activists were likely to face an all-white jury in a part of the country where anti-Indian sentiment ran high. It was not uncommon for high profile trials involving Native Americans in the northwest to be moved to Los Angeles or other urban areas, where Native Americans were more likely to be treated fairly.

- Al Bridges (1922–1982) and Hank Adams (1944–), mentioned at the end of this report as being targeted by angry game wardens, were two of the earliest leaders of the fish-ins. Bridges was a Nisqually Indian from Gig Harbor, Washington; Adams is an Assiniboine-Dakota Indian from Poplar, Montana, and was a leader of the National Indian Youth Council in the 1960s.

"The New Indian Wars"

*On October 13, 1965, we held a "**fish-in**" on the Nisqually River to try and bring a focus on our fishing fight with the State of Washington. The "fish-in" started at 4:00 P.M. and was over at about 4:30 P.M. It ended with six Indians in jail and dazed Indian kids wondering "what happened?"*

My parents, Don and Janet McCloud; Al and Maiselle Bridges; Suzan Satiacum and Don George, Jr., were arrested that day. They were released after posting bail a few hours later. The charges against these six Indians was "obstructing the duty of a police officer." Now all we could do was wait till the trials started. There was a seventh Indian who was later arrested for the same charge, Nugent Kautz. And he had not been at Frank's Landing on that day.

The trial was to begin on January 15, 1969, at 9:30 A.M. We went into the courthouse that Wednesday certain that we would not receive justice as was proven to us in other trials. As we walked into the hallways there were many game wardens standing there, some dressed in their uniforms and some in plain clothes, but we recognized all of them.

Many of us were dressed in our traditional way with headbands, leggings and necklaces. As we walked the length of the corridor to the courtroom, the game wardens were looking us up and down, laughing at us. I said to my cousin, "Don't pay any attention to them, they don't know any better" ....

The first witness for the State was a field marshal for the game department—Zimmerman. He stated that he was directing the game wardens at the Landing on Oct. 13. He was in charge of the reinforcements from all over the State that came down on us like a sea of green. At the time of the fish-in I thought that there were about a hundred game wardens.

The next State witness was the public relations man for the game department. He had 16 millimeter motion pictures to show. He had been posing as a newsman on the day of the fish-in. Our attorney objected to the pictures because they could have been cut and fixed to the State's advantage or taken for the State's advantage. But the State got their way and the motion pictures were shown. And to this

Fish-in: Form of civil disobedience in which Indian activists fished in violation of state laws, in order to assert their treaty rights. This tactic was used in the 1960s and 1970s in Washington and Oregon.

moment I can not understand why they wanted these pictures shown because they sure looked better for our side than for theirs....

The next morning the State started off with their last witness, State Fisheries Biologist, Lasseter. He talked about how we Indians are the ones who depleted the fish in the Puyallup River and if we weren't controlled we would do the same to the Nisqually River. The Puyallup River is filled with pollution more than it is with water. And why would we want to wipe out our livelihood? Our attorney made Lasseter state that it could have been the pollution not the Indians who depleted the fish in the Puyallup River.

Now, it was our turn! The first witness for our defense was Bob Johnson. At the time of the fish-in he was the editor of the "Auburn Citizen" newspaper. He told of the tactics the game wardens used on us. Mr. Johnson also had evidence with him, pictures of the game wardens, showing **billie clubs** and **seven-celled flashlights.**

The Prosecuting attorney got real shook up about these. It seemed like he was saying "I object" every few minutes....

The next defense witness was Janet McCloud, Tulalip Indian. She told the facts about why the Indians had had the fish-in demonstration on that day and what the mood the Indians had before the fish-in. This was important because the State thought we were after blood that day. And we were not expecting any violence because all my brothers and sisters were there and the youngest was four at that time. And if we had expected any violence none of the children would have been there. She told how she felt when she realized that the game wardens were going to ram our boat and how she felt when she realized these men meant business with their seven-celled flashlights, billie clubs, and **brass knuckles.**

My two little brothers were in that boat when it was rammed, the youngest was seven and could not swim. Besides, once you get tangled in nylon mesh it is very easy to drown. While she was telling this story, we could tell she was trying very hard to keep from crying, but this did not help because she started to. And every Indian in that courtroom that was there that horrible day started to remember the fear and anger that they had felt that day....

The next witness was Don McCloud, Puyallup Indian. He was one of the Indian men in the boat that day. He told how the boat was rammed. (Oh, incidentally, the game wardens said that they did not ram the boat.) He also said how he had seen a game warden with a steel pipe and how a game warden tried to knee him in the groin. And

Billie clubs: Long, thin wooden clubs, often used by police and law enforcement officials.

Seven-celled flashlight: Powerful, metal flashlight requiring seven "D"-cell batteries, that is long and heavy and may be used as a weapon.

Brass knuckles: Weapon used to increase the power of a punch. It is a band of metal with four finger holes that fits over the knuckles.

Janet McCloud

Janet McCloud, a Tulalip/Nisqually Indian and a direct descendent of Chief Seattle (1788–1866), was born in northwestern Washington state in 1935. She has fought for Native American rights through all of her adult life. In the 1960s and 1970s McCloud was a leader in the movement for Indian fishing rights. She and her husband were arrested many times during fish-ins (protests in which participants fished in violation of state laws, to assert their treaty rights). She has also served as spokesperson for the Nisqually nation.

McCloud joined the American Indian Movement (AIM), a militant Indian rights organization, in the early 1970s. In the late 1970s McCloud was a founder of Women of All Red Nations (WARN)—a women's group within AIM that worked to end domestic violence in Indian communities. In 1978 McCloud participated in AIM's Longest Walk march from San Francisco to Washington, D.C., in which activists demanded sovereignty (self-governance) for all Indian nations. McCloud has also been active in fighting anti-Indian discrimination in the school district of Yelm, Washington, on the outskirts of the Nisqually Reservation, where her eight children were educated.

Now a grandmother of twenty-four, McCloud serves as a spiritual counselor for Native American women. "Don't neglect the spiritual part of your life," stated McCloud in an interview in the 1995 book *Messengers of the Wind: Native American Women Tell Their Life Stories*. "If you get all locked up in the white man's world, you'll start to wither inside. People turn to drugs or alcohol because their spirit isn't being fed."

the other acts of violence that he had witnessed the game wardens doing....

With all this testimony and evidence, it was plain to see that the game wardens had lied. We only hoped that the jury would believe our side of the fish-in story. We also learned the names of the game wardens whose pictures we had, especially the one who had been beating on Alison and Valerie Bridges.

Mr. Zionitz called one last witness—a hostile one—a game warden. This was the one who had been carrying a leather slapper which the Indians confiscated on 1/13/65 from his hip-pocket and had entered as evidence. His name was engraved on the slapper. He admitted that it was his and had been taken out his pocket but he said that he never used it.

The State called "Colonel Custer" Neubrech for their rebuttal witness. He said at the briefing he had given his men the night before the fish-in he had told them to have extreme patience with the Indians. Either they don't know the meaning of extreme patience or else they didn't understand him right....

After the two lawyers gave their summations the jury went into session. This was at ten o'clock at night. They were out until midnight. The foreman came in first and said, "The rest are afraid to come in." I thought, here comes another guilty. When the foreman handed the judge the decision the room became very silent. Then the judge read, "The jury finds the defendant Nugent Kautz 'not guilty'" He read the rest of the names with the same verdict. I did't believe it. I turned to my cousin and said, "Did I hear right?" She nodded her head, yes. Everyone was happy, except for the State. The game wardens were very hostile after this.

Footnote: The game wardens, incensed at the adverse verdict, left the Tyee Motel where they had been celebrating, prematurely, their victory and went down in large numbers to Frank's Landing. A sympathetic soul overheard the wardens and called the Landing to warn the Indians. Nevertheless the wardens caught a car load of Indians at the railroad trestle and surrounded them in their state game cars—they proceeded to hit the Indians' car with their nightsticks, cussing them and trying to provoke Al Bridges and Hank Adams to fight. It was obvious to the Indians that they had been drinking.... So the war goes on—which goes to prove that the history books are wrong when they talk about "the last Indian wars." They have never stopped!

Laura McCloud, Tulalip (Nabokov, pp. 362–66)

What happened next...

Native American fishing rights activists were handed a victory in 1974, with the decision in the landmark court case *United States v. Washington.* Judge George H. Boldt (1903–) of the Federal Court for the District of Washington State ruled that Native Americans were entitled to catch up to 50 percent of the fish in the Puget Sound area—the traditional fishing region of the northwestern tribes at the time they signed treaties (the 1850s).

"Because the right of each Treaty Tribe to take anadromous [fish that migrate from the ocean up a river to spawn, or mate, such as salmon] fish arises from a treaty with the United States," Boldt wrote in his ruling, "that right is preserved and protected under the supreme law of the land, does not depend on State law, is distinct from rights or privileges held by others, and may not be qualified by any action of the State." Boldt's decision was twice upheld by the Supreme Court, which refused to hear appeals in the matter.

State legislators, law enforcement officials, and non-Indian fishermen responded angrily to Judge Boldt's decision. Boldt was accused of being insane, of having accepted bribes by the Indians, and of having an Indian mistress (none of the accusations was true). White fisherman hung an effigy (a mannequin that looked like Boldt) of Boldt and put bumper-stickers on their cars reading "Can Judge Boldt." They also vandalized Coast Guard vessels that were sent to the area to enforce Boldt's decision and shot at least one Coast Guard official. Indian fisherman, under constant threat of physical attack, were forced to arm themselves.

The fears of white commercial fishermen that the Boldt ruling would ruin their operations turned out to be baseless. Following the ruling, Indians did not catch anywhere near the 50 percent of fish allowed by law. From the years 1974 through 1977, Native Americans took between 7 and 25 percent of the catch. Nonetheless, battles over fishing rights continued in Washington through the 1980s.

Did you know...

- Actor Marlon Brando (1924–) has a long history of supporting Native American rights. Brando participated in fish-ins (he was arrested in one case) and demonstrations in favor of Indian fishing rights in the 1960s. In 1973, while Indian activists were occupying the hamlet of Wounded Knee on the Pine Ridge Reservation in South Dakota, Brando refused to accept an Academy Award for his performance in *The Godfather*. Brando instead issued a statement condemning Hollywood's racist portrayal of Native Americans in movies.

- Janet McCloud advocated that Native American history be taught in schools, long before the adoption of Indian studies and other ethnic studies programs in the early 1970s.

Sources

Books

Grossman, Mark. *The ABC-CLIO Companion to the American Indian Rights Movement*. Santa Barbara, CA: ABC-CLIO, 1996.

Johansen, Bruce E., and Donald A. Grinde, Jr. *The Encyclopedia of Native American Biography: Six Hundred Life Stories of Important People from Powhatan to Wilma Mankiller*. New York: Da Capo Press, 1988.

Josephy, Alvin M., Jr., ed. *Red Power: The American Indians' Fight for Freedom*. New York: McGraw-Hill Book Company, 1971.

Katz, Jane, ed. *Messengers of the Wind: Native American Women Tell Their Life Stories*. New York: Ballantine Books, 1995, pp. 272–83.

Lyons, Oren R., and John C. Mohawk, eds. *Exiled in the Land of the Free: Democracy, Indian Nations, and the U.S. Constitution*. Santa Fe: Clear Light Publishers, 1992.

Nabakov, Peter, ed. *Native America Testimony: A Chronicle of Indian-White Relations from Prophecy to the Present, 1492–1992*. New York: Viking, 1991.

Olson, James S. *Encyclopedia of American Indian Civil Rights*. Westport, CT: Greenwood Press, 1997.

Human Rights

3

Human rights are loosely defined as guarantees of freedom and equality as applied to individuals and certain groups of people (based on race, ethnicity, gender, or other criteria). Human rights can also be thought of as freedom from exploitation, oppression, and persecution. The United Nations (UN), in its Universal Declaration of Human Rights (written in 1948), includes as human rights the right to life, liberty, education, and equality before the law, as well as the freedom of movement, religion, association, and information. The writings in this chapter each touch on specific aspects of human rights as applied to specific groups of people in the United States.

Malcolm X (1925–1965) was a powerful and controversial advocate for the human rights of African Americans. Through his fiery orations, Malcolm X exposed the evils of racism. He urged black people to defend themselves and to strive toward political, economic, and social self-sufficiency. Malcolm X also appealed to the UN to pressure the U. S. government to respect the human rights of its black citizens.

One of the greatest defenders of the human rights of Hispanic Americans was **Rodolfo "Corky" Gonzales** (1929–).

A civil rights protester is attacked in Birmingham, Alabama.
Reproduced by permission of AP/Wide World Photos.

Gonzales brought together Mexican Americans to fight against police brutality and discrimination in the public schools in the late 1960s and early 1970s. In his epic poem *I Am Joaquín*, Gonzales denounced the abuse of Mexican Americans' human rights and inspired a spiritual and cultural awakening in his people.

The struggle for Native American human rights in the late 1960s and 1970s was led by the American Indian Movement (AIM). AIM used confrontational tactics to highlight the injustices inflicted on the Indian people by U.S. government policies. The group also sought improvements to the abysmal living conditions of Indians on reservations and in cities. As AIM activist **Vernon Bellecourt** explains in "The Birth of AIM," the original mission of AIM was to stop police brutality against Native Americans in Minneapolis. That mission rapidly expanded to encompass a range of human rights issues.

One of the most blatant human rights violations in U.S. history was the internment of Japanese Americans during World War II. Between the years 1942 and 1945, approximately 120,000 people of Japanese descent were imprisoned in relocation camps (sometimes referred to as concentration camps). This relocation policy was largely a reaction to the bombing of Pearl Harbor, Hawaii, by Japanese forces on December 7, 1941. The internment was carried out despite a lack of any evidence of disloyalty to the United States on the part of Japanese Americans; in fact, it was later determined that there had been no military necessity for the incarceration.

In 1981, the **Commission on Wartime Relocation and Internment of Civilians** was established by Congress to assess the harm caused by the internment of Japanese Americans during World War II. After hearing testimony from more than 750 witnesses—many of them former detainees—the commission issued its report, *Personal Justice Denied*. The report was a scathing indictment of the decision to imprison Japanese Americans. The committee concluded that the wartime treatment of Japanese Americans had been guided by war hysteria and racial prejudice.

For much of American history, the human rights of women have not been respected. Until the mid-1800s, women could not own property and did not have legal guardianship over their children. Until 1920, women did not have the right to vote. An argument as to why women deserve the right to vote is outlined by the **National American Woman Suffrage Association (NAWSA)** in its "Declaration of Principles."

Lesbians and gay men constitute another group of Americans whose human rights have been and continue to be abridged. At present there is no federal legislation guaranteeing the rights of homosexuals. Gay men and lesbians are frequent victims of hate crimes, same-sex marriage is prohibited by federal government statute, and discrimination based on sexual orientation in employment and housing is widespread. In this chapter, four prominent civic leaders lend their voices to the chorus demanding the respect of human rights of lesbians and gay men.

Until 1990 there was no sweeping federal policy guaranteeing the human rights of people with disabilities. Even since the passage of the Americans with Disabilities Act, people with disabilities continue to face widespread discrimination in employment, housing, and education. In the "Disabled Peoples' Bill of Rights" the **American Coalition of Citizens with Disabilities** calls for the full acceptance of people with disabilities into the mainstream of American society.

AIM activist Russell Means (standing) at a 1970 Native American rights rally.
Reproduced by permission of AP/Wide World Photos.

Malcolm X

"See for Yourself, Listen for Yourself, Think for Yourself"

Speech delivered on January 1, 1965
Reprinted in *Malcolm X Talks to Young People:*
Speeches in the U.S., Britain and Africa
Published in 1965

Malcolm X was a powerful and controversial advocate for the rights of African Americans. Through his passionate and provocative speeches, Malcolm X expressed the anger and frustration that most African Americans felt about racism. As national spokesperson for the black Muslim group Nation of Islam (NOI) from 1952 to 1963, Malcolm X inspired black people in the North in much the same way that Martin Luther King Jr. (1929–1968), did in the South. There was a wide gulf, however, between the philosophies of the two leaders. While King advocated nonviolence (the rejection of all forms of violence) and integration, Malcolm X stressed the need for African Americans to defend themselves and to form their own institutions.

One of the South's most prominent civil rights groups and one of the best examples of an organization that practiced nonviolence was the Student Nonviolent Coordinating Committee (SNCC; pronounced "snick"). The SNCC was formed by students who were active in the 1960 lunch counter desegregation movement. SNCC members understood all too well the consequences of nonviolence.

"One of the first things I think young people ... should learn how to do is see for yourself and listen for yourself and think for yourself. Then you can come to an intelligent decision for yourself."

From 1960 through 1964 the young people of the SNCC fought for desegregation and attempted to register black voters in the most segregated regions of the South. (Blacks were kept from voting by literacy tests [difficult tests in which applicants had to read and interpret portions of the state constitution to the satisfaction of the registrar], poll taxes [a tax black voters had to pay—and be able to prove that they had paid—in order to vote], threats of home eviction and job loss, and outright violence.) The SNCC's most dangerous work took place in Mississippi, the state that in the early 1960s led the South in the number of lynchings, beatings, and unexplained disappearances of African Americans. Numerous SNCC workers in Mississippi and in other parts of the South had been arrested and, in many cases, beaten; some had even been killed.

As 1964 drew to a close, many members of the SNCC were rethinking their commitment to nonviolence. The physical beatings and intimidation they had endured had taken a great physical and emotional toll. Many SNCC members decided that trying to win over their foes with moral persuasion was futile; some began carrying guns. The philosophy of the SNCC as an organization was shifting away from that of Martin Luther King Jr., and toward that of Malcolm X.

At the end of 1964 the SNCC sent a group of young activists from McComb, Mississippi, on an eight-day study trip to New York. McComb was where SNCC had initiated its Mississippi voter registration project in 1960. It was also the site of an SNCC-led demonstration, in which 100 McComb high school students had marched to the city hall to protest the 1961 killing of farmer and civil rights activist Herbert Lee. On January 1, 1965, Malcolm X made the following address to the members of the McComb delegation.

Things to remember while reading "See for Yourself, Listen for Yourself, Think for Yourself":

- Malcolm X rejected the concept of nonviolent action, believing that the meaning of nonviolence was lost on unabashed and violent racists. Malcolm X was diametrically opposed to most civil rights leaders, most notably Martin Luther King Jr., on the question of nonviolence. King preached that violence cannot be overcome by violence, and that only love can conquer hate. He called upon civil rights activists not to strike back against their oppressors. Malcolm X was famous for stating, "if someone puts a hand on you, send him to the cemetery."

- Malcolm X makes several references to the violence of the Ku Klux Klan. The Klan and other white supremacist groups (such as the Knights of White Camelia and the Black Legionnaires) had subjected African Americans to lynchings and other forms of violence since the latter half of the nineteenth century. (Lynching is the execution-style murder of a black person, often by hanging, by a white mob.) A total of 4,742 black Americans had been lynched between the years 1882 and 1964.

- Malcolm X criticizes black labor leader A. Philip Randolph (1889–1979) for having demanded that blacks be given equal opportunity to serve in the armed forces during World War II (1939–45). Randolph's greatest claim to fame during that era was his fight to end discrimination against black workers in defense-related industries. Randolph threatened to lead tens of thousands of black workers in a protest march on the nation's capital in July 1941 if black workers continued to be shunted into low-paying positions. Six days before the planned march, President Franklin Delano Roosevelt (1882–1945) gave in, signing a presidential order prohibiting job discrimination in defense-related industries with government contracts.

- Malcolm X journeyed through the Middle East and Africa in the spring of 1964. On that trip he met African politicians and citizens who were concerned with the plight of black Americans. Malcolm X became convinced that black Americans, rather than look to white U.S. government officials for help, should appeal to the United Nations (UN). Malcolm X believed that the UN would pressure the United States to respect the human rights of its black citizens.

"See for Yourself, Listen for Yourself, Think for Yourself"

One of the first things I think young people, especially nowadays, should learn how to do is see for yourself and listen for yourself and think for yourself. Then you can come to an intelligent decision for yourself. But if you form the habit of going by what you hear others say about someone, or going by what others think about someone, instead of going and searching that thing out for yourself and seeing for yourself, you'll be walking west when you think you're going east, and you'll be walking east when you think you're going west. So this generation, especially of our people, have a burden upon themselves, more so than at any other time in history. The most important thing we can learn how to do today is think for ourselves.

It's good to keep wide-open ears and listen to what everybody else has to say, but when you come to make a decision, you have to weigh all of what you've heard on its own, and place it where it belongs, and then come to a decision for yourself. You'll never regret it. But if you form the habit of taking what someone else says about a thing without checking it out for yourself, you'll find that other people will have you hating your own friends and loving your enemies. This is one of the things that our people are beginning to learn today—that it is very important to think out a situation for yourself. If you don't do it, then you'll always be maneuvered into actually—You'll never fight your enemies, but you will find yourself fighting your own self.

I think our people in this country are the best examples of that. Because many of us want to be nonviolent. We talk very loudly, you know, about being nonviolent. Here in Harlem, where there are probably more Black people concentrated than any place else in the world, some talk that nonviolent talk too. And when they stop talking about how nonviolent they are, we find that they aren't nonviolent with each other. At Harlem Hospital, you can go out here on Friday night, which—today is what, Friday? yes—you can go out here to Harlem Hospital, where there are more Black patients in one hospital than any hospital in the world—because there's a concentration of our people here—and find Black people who claim they're nonviolent. But you see them going in there all cut up and shot up and busted up where they got violent with each other.

So my experience has been that in many instances where you find Negroes always talking about being nonviolent, they're not nonviolent with each other, and they're not loving with each other, or patient with each other, or forgiving with each other. Usually, when they say they're nonviolent, they mean they're nonviolent with somebody else. I think you understand what I mean. They are nonviolent with the enemy. A person can come to your home, and if he's white and he wants to heap some kind of brutality upon you, you're nonviolent. Or he can come put a rope around your neck, you're nonviolent. Or he can come to take your father out and put a rope around his neck, you're nonviolent. But now if another Negro just stomps his foot, you'll rumble with him in a minute. Which shows you there's an inconsistency there.

So I myself would go for **nonviolence** if it was consistent, if it was intelligent, if everybody was going to be nonviolent, and if we were going to be nonviolent all the time. I'd say, okay, let's get with it, we'll all be nonviolent. But I don't go along—and I'm just telling you how I think—I don't go along with any kind of nonviolence unless everybody's going to be nonviolent. If they make the **Ku Klux Klan** nonviolent, I'll be nonviolent. If they make the **White Citizens' Council** nonviolent, I'll be nonviolent. But as long as you've got somebody else not being nonviolent, I don't want anybody coming to me talking any kind of nonviolent talk. I don't think it is fair to tell our people to be nonviolent unless someone is out there making the Klan and the Citizens' Council and these other groups also be nonviolent.

Now I'm not criticizing those here who are nonviolent. I think everybody should do it the way they feel is best, and I congratulate anybody who can be nonviolent in the face of all that kind of action that I read about in that part of the world. But I don't think that in 1965 you will find the upcoming generation of our people, especially those who have been doing some thinking, who will go along with any form of nonviolence unless nonviolence is going to be practiced all the way around.

If the leaders of the nonviolent movement can go into the white community and teach nonviolence, good. I'd go along with that. But as long as I see them teaching nonviolence only in the Black community, then we can't go along with that. We believe in equality, and equality means you have to put the same thing over here that you put over there. And if just Black people alone are going to be the ones who are nonviolent, then it's not fair. We throw ourselves off guard. In fact, we disarm ourselves and make ourselves defenseless....

Nonviolence: The rejection of all forms of violence, especially while protesting injustices.

Ku Klux Klan: Southern anti-black terrorist group formed after the Civil War (1861–65).

White Citizens' Council: Organization of white businessmen and professionals that worked to forestall the political and economic advancement of African Americans in the South from the 1950s through the 1970s.

*The **Organization of Afro-American Unity** is a nonreligious group of Black people in this country who believe that the problems confronting our people in this country need to be reanalyzed and a new approach devised toward trying to get a solution. Studying the problem, we recall that prior to 1939 in this country, all of our people—in the North, South, East, and West, no matter how much education we had—were segregated.*

*We were segregated in the North just as much as we were segregated in the South. And even right now, today, there's as much **segregation** in the North as there is in the South. There's some worse segregation right here in New York City than there is in McComb, Mississippi; but up here they're subtle and tricky and deceitful, and they make you think that you've got it made when you haven't even begun to make it yet.*

*Prior to 1939 our people were in a very **menial** position or condition. Most of us were waiters and porters and bellhops and janitors and waitresses and things of that sort. It was not until war was declared in Germany by **Hitler,** and America became involved in a manpower shortage in regards to her factories plus her army—it was only then that the Black man in this country was permitted to make a few strides forwards. It was never out of some kind of moral enlightenment or moral awareness on the part of **Uncle Sam.** Uncle Sam only let the Black man take a step forward when he himself had his back to the wall.*

In Michigan, where I was brought up at that time, I recall that the best jobs in the city for Blacks were waiters out at the country club. And in those days if you had a job waiting table in the country club, you had it made. Or if you had a job at the State House. Having a job at the State House didn't mean that you were a clerk or something of that sort—you had the shoeshine stand in the State House. Just by being in there where you could be around all these big politicians, that made you a big-shot Negro. You were shining shoes, but you were a big-shot Negro because you were around big-shot white people and you could bend their ear and get up next to them. And ofttimes in those days, you were chosen to be the voice of the Negro community.

Also right at this time, 1939 or '40, '41, they weren't drafting Negroes in the army or the navy. A Negro couldn't join the navy in 1940 or '41 in this country. He couldn't join. They wouldn't take a Black man in the navy. They would take him if they wanted and make him a cook. But he couldn't just go and join the navy. And he couldn't just go—I don't think he could just go and join the army. They weren't drafting him when the war first started.

This is what they thought of you and me in those days. For one thing, they didn't trust us. They feared that if they put us in the army and trained us on how to use rifles and other things, that we might shoot at some targets that they hadn't picked out. And we would have. Any thinking man knows what target to shoot at. And if a man doesn't, if he has to have someone else to choose his target, then he's not thinking for himself—they're doing the thinking for him.

*So it was only when the Negro leaders—they had the same type of Negro leaders in those days that we have today—when the Negro leaders saw all the white fellows being drafted and taken into the army and dying on the battlefield, and no Negroes were dying because they weren't being drafted, the Negro leaders came up and said, "We've got to die too. We want to be drafted too, and we demand that you take us in there and let us die for our country too." This is what the Negro leaders said, back in 1940, I remember. A. Philip Randolph was one of the leading Negroes in those days who said it, and he's one of the **Big Six** right now; and this is why he's one of the Big Six right now.*

*They started drafting Negro soldiers then, and then they started letting Negroes get into the navy—but not until Hitler and **Tojo** and the foreign powers were strong enough to bring pressure upon this country, so that it had its back to the wall and it needed us. At that same time, they let us work in factories. Up until that time we couldn't work in the factories. I'm talking about the North as well as the South. And when they let us work in the factories we began—at first when they let us in we could only be janitors. Then, after a year or so passed by, they let us work on machines. We became machinists, got a little skill. And as we got a little more skill, we made a little more money, which enabled us to live in a little better neighborhood. When we lived in a little better neighborhood, we went to a little better school, got a little better education, and could come out and get a little better job. So the cycle was broken somewhat....*

Now the point that I'm making is this: Never at any time in the history of our people in this country have we made advances or advancement, or made progress in any way just based upon the internal good will of this country, or based upon the internal activity of this country. We have only made advancement in this country when this country was under pressure from forces above and beyond its control. Because the internal moral consciousness of this country is bankrupt.

Big Six: The heads of the six most prominent civil rights organizations in the United States in the early 1960s: Martin Luther King Jr., president of the Southern Christian Leadership Conference; A. Philip Randolph, founder of the Brotherhood of Sleeping Car Porters; Roy Wilkins, president of the National Association for the Advancement of Colored People; Jim Farmer, chairman of the Congress on Racial Equality; Whitney Young, president of the National Urban League; and John Lewis, chair of the Student Nonviolent Coordinating Committee.

Hideki Tojo: 1884–1948; Japanese prime minister during World War II.

Malcolm X

Malcolm X was born Malcolm Little in Nebraska in 1925. When he was four years old, his home was set afire by Ku Klux Klan members. After that attack, the Little family moved to Milwaukee, Wisconsin, and then to Lansing, Michigan. In 1961 Malcolm's father, a Baptist preacher, was killed—allegedly by members of a white supremacist group called the Black Legionnaires.

Malcolm X excelled in his studies as a youngster but was discouraged from pursuing academics by racist school counselors. Malcolm dropped out of school in the eighth grade and soon thereafter got involved in street crime. He was convicted of burglary in Massachusetts in 1946 and sentenced to serve time in prison.

While in prison, Malcolm X joined the black Muslim group the Nation of Islam (NOI). The NOI mandated a strict regimen of prayer and self-discipline and taught that blacks were superior to whites. Upon his release from prison in 1952, Malcolm X replaced the name "Little" with "X." "Little" was the name given to Malcolm's great-grandparents, who were slaves, by their owner. "X" stood for the unknown surname of Malcolm's African ancestors.

Malcolm X began preaching on street corners in Harlem, New York. He rapidly rose to fame for his fiery oratory style and his strident message of hatred toward

Malcolm X. *Reproduced by permission of AP/Wide World Photos.*

white America and pride in black America. From 1952 to 1963 Malcolm X served as national spokesperson for the NOI.

In the spring of 1964, after breaking with NOI leader Elijah Muhammad (1897–1975), Malcolm X traveled to the Middle East on a prayer pilgrimage. There he lived and prayed with Muslims of all races. That experience made Malcolm X reject the NOI definition of white people as "blue-eyed devils."

Malcolm X was shot to death on February 21, 1965, by three men with ties to the NOI, as he spoke before a huge crowd in Harlem's Audubon Ballroom.

It hasn't existed since they first brought us over here and made slaves out of us. They trick up on the confirmation and make it appear that they have our good interests at heart. But when you study it, every time, no matter how many steps they take us forward, it's like we're standing on a—what do you call that thing?—a treadmill. The treadmill is moving backwards faster then we're able to go forward in this direction. We're not even standing still—we're walking forward, at the same time we're going backward.

I say that because of the Organization of Afro-American Unity, in studying the process of this so-called progress during the past twenty years, realized that the only time the Black man in this country is given any kind of recognition, or shown any kind of favor at all, or even his voice is listened to, is when America is afraid of outside pressure, or when she's afraid of her image abroad. We could see that as long as we sat around and carried on our struggle at a level or in a manner that involved only the good will of the internal forces of this country, we would continue to go backward, there would be no real meaningful changes made. So the Organization of Afro-American Unity saw that it was necessary to expand the problem and the struggle of the Black man in this country until it went above and beyond the **jurisdiction** of the United States.

For the past fifteen years the struggle of the Black man in this country was labeled as a civil rights struggle, and as such it remained completely within the jurisdiction of the United States. You and I could get no kind of benefits whatsoever other than that which would be forthcoming from Washington, D.C. Which meant, in order for it to be forthcoming from Washington, D.C., all of the congressmen and the senators would have to agree to it.

But the most powerful congressmen and the most powerful senators were from the South. And they were from the South because they had seniority in Washington, D.C. And they had seniority because our people in the South, where they came from, couldn't vote. They didn't have the right to vote.

So when we saw that we were up against a hopeless battle internally, we saw the necessity of getting allies at the world level or from abroad, from all over the world. And so immediately we realized that as long as the struggle was a civil rights struggle, was under the jurisdiction of the United States, we would have no real allies or real support. We decided that the only way to make the problem rise to the level where we could get world support was to take it away from the civil rights label, and put in the human rights label....

Jurisdiction: The range or extent of authority or legal control.

*When you get involved in a struggle for human rights, it's completely out of the jurisdiction of the United States government. You take it to the **United Nations**. And any problem that is taken to the United Nations, the United States has no say-so on it whatsoever. Because in the UN she only has one vote, and in the UN the largest bloc of votes is African; the continent of Africa has the largest bloc of votes of any continent on this earth. And the continent of Africa, coupled with the Asian bloc and the Arab bloc, comprises over two-thirds of the UN forces, and they're the dark nations. That's the only court that you can go to today and get your own people, the people who look like you, on your side—the United Nations....*

*And today you'll find in the United Nations—and it's not an accident—that every time the Congo question or anything on the African continent is being debated in the Security Council, they couple it with what's going on, or what is happening to you and me, in Mississippi and Alabama and these other places. In my opinion, the greatest accomplishment that was made in the struggle of the Black man in America in 1964 toward some kind of real progress was the successful linking together of our problem with the African problem, or making our problem a world problem. Because now, whenever anything happens to you in Mississippi, it's not a case of just somebody in Alabama getting indignant, or somebody in New York getting indignant. Whatever happens in Mississippi today, with the attention of the African nations drawn toward Mississippi at a governmental level, then the same **repercussions** that you see all over the world when an imperialist or foreign power interferes in some section of Africa, you see repercussions, you see the embassies being bombed and burned and overturned. Nowadays, when something happens to Black people in Mississippi, you will see the same repercussions all over the world.*

I wanted to point this out to you, because it is important for you to know that when you're in Mississippi you're not alone. But as long as you think you're alone, then you take a stand as if you're a minority or as if you're out-numbered, and that kind of stand will never enable you to win a battle. You've got to know that you've got as much power on your side as that Ku Klux Klan has on its side. And when you know that you've got just as much power on your side as the Klan has on its side, you'll talk the same kind of language with that Klan as that Klan is talking with you.

I'll say one more thing, and then I'll conclude.

When I say the same kind of language, I should explain what I mean. See, you can never get good relations with anybody that you

United Nations: Full name, United Nations Security Council. The most powerful decision-making body of the United Nations, consisting of five permanent members: the United States, Russia, China, France, and Great Britain. Ten other nations each serve on the security body for two-year elected terms.

Repercussions: Usually negative effects of an action.

can't communicate with. You can never have good relations with anybody that doesn't understand you. There has to be an understanding. Understanding is brought about through dialogue. Dialogue is communication of ideas. This can only be done in a language, a common language. You can never talk French to somebody who speaks only German and think you're communicating. Neither of them—they don't get the point. You have to be able to speak a man's language in order to make him get the point.

Now, you've lived in Mississippi long enough to know what the language of the Ku Klux Klan is. They only know one language. If you come up with another language, you don't communicate. You've got to be able to speak the same language they speak, whether you're in Mississippi, New York City, or Alabama, or California, or anywhere else. When you develop or mature to the point where you can speak another man's language on his level, that man gets the point. That's the only time he gets the point. You can't talk peace to a person who doesn't know what peace means. You can't talk love to a person who doesn't know what love means. And you can't talk any form of nonviolence to a person who doesn't believe in nonviolence. Why, you're wasting your time.

So I think in 1965—whether you like it, or I like it, or we like it, or they like it, or not—you will see that there is a generation of Black people born in this country who become mature to the point where they feel that they have no more business being asked to take a peaceful approach than anybody else takes, unless everybody's going to take a peaceful approach.

So we here in the Organization of Afro-American Unity, we're with the struggle in Mississippi 1,000 percent. We're with the efforts to register our people in Mississippi to vote 1,000 percent. But we do not go along with anybody telling us to help nonviolently. We think if the government says that Negroes have a right to vote, and then when Negroes go out to vote some kind of Ku Klux Klan is going to put them in the river, and the government doesn't do anything about it, it's time for us to organize and band together and equip ourselves and qualify ourselves to protect ourselves. [Applause] And once you can protect yourself, you don't have to worry about being hurt. That's it. [Applause]. (Clark, pp. 49–51, 53–55, 56–58, 60–62)

Malcolm X (on stretcher) was shot to death on February 21, 1965, as he spoke to his followers at the Audubon Ballroom in Harlem, New York.
Reproduced by permission of Corbis-Bettmann.

What happened next...

One month after Malcolm X addressed the Mississippi youth group in Harlem, he headed to Selma, Alabama. Malcolm X had been invited by the SNCC to speak to Selma residents who were engaged in an historic voter registration drive. Malcolm X spoke in Selma on February 4, 1965—the same day that President Johnson introduced his voting rights bill in Congress. (That bill was signed into law as the Voting Rights Act on August 6, 1965; the legislation outlawed all practices used to deny blacks the right to vote and empowered federal registrars to register black voters.)

"The white people should thank Dr. King for holding people in check," Malcolm X told an overflow audience in Brown's chapel. "For there are other [black leaders] who do not believe in these [nonviolent] measures."

On the day Malcolm X spoke, Martin Luther King Jr. was in jail for his part in a civil rights demonstration. "I want Dr. King to know," Malcolm X told King's wife, Coretta Scott

King, "that I didn't come to Selma to make his job difficult.... If the white people realize what the alternative is, perhaps they will be more willing to hear Dr. King."

Malcolm X was assassinated seventeen days after his speech in Selma. Tensions between Malcolm X and the NOI had been growing ever since Malcolm X had left the organization in early 1964. NOI faithfuls feared losing their base of support to Malcolm X. They were also angry over Malcolm X's labeling of Elijah Muhammad as a "racist" and a "political fakir."

Malcolm X's house was firebombed on February 14, 1965, allegedly by NOI members. One week later he was shot to death in Harlem's Audubon Ballroom as he spoke to his followers. While three men with ties to the NOI were convicted of the murder, there is speculation that the Federal Bureau of Investigation (FBI) played a role in the assassination plot.

The influence of Malcolm X did not end with his death. To the contrary, shortly after Malcolm X's assassination there was a sharp increase in the level of militancy among black activists in America. The traditional anthem of the civil rights movement, "We Shall Overcome," was replaced by cries of "Black Power!" The notion of black power was similar to the teachings of Malcolm X in that it proclaimed that blacks did not have to ask whites for acceptance, and that blacks held the power to create a better society for themselves.

Did you know...

- Malcolm X's 1964 pilgrimage to the holy land of Mecca, Saudi Arabia, led him to convert to orthodox Islam and change his name to El-Hajj Malik El-Shabazz.

- The Federal Bureau of Investigation (FBI), as part of its program to destroy black nationalist groups in the 1960s, used undercover agents to fan the flames of rivalry between Malcolm X and Elijah Muhammad. There is evidence that FBI agents encouraged three fanatical followers of Muhammad to assassinate Malcolm X.

- In 1999 the U.S. government honored Malcolm X by placing his image on a 33-cent postage stamp.

Sources
Books

African American Biography. Vol. 3. Detroit: U•X•L, 1994, pp. 487–90.

Clark, Steven, ed. *Malcolm X Talks to Young People: Speeches in the U.S., Britain and Africa.* New York: Pathfinder Press, 1965.

Levy, Peter B. *The Civil Rights Movement.* Westwood, CT: Greenwood Press, 1998.

Malcolm X (with Alex Haley). *The Autobiography of Malcolm X.* New York: Grove Press, 1965.

O'Reilly, Kenneth. *Black Americans: The FBI Files.* New York: Carroll and Graf Publishers, Inc., 1994.

Smallwood, David, et al. *Profiles of Great African Americans.* Lincolnwood, IL: Publications International, Ltd., 1996, pp. 208–11.

Williams, Juan. *Eyes on the Prize: America's Civil Rights Years, 1954–1965.* New York: Penguin Books, 1987.

Rodolfo "Corky" Gonzales

I Am Joaquín

Excerpt from *I Am Joaquín/Yo Soy Joaquín*
Published in 1972

U rban Mexican American youth underwent a great political and social awakening during the years 1967 to 1971. Inspired by the African American civil rights movement, the movement to end the war in Vietnam (1954–75), and the Hispanic farm workers' struggle for justice in the fields of California, the young people began to fight for their own rights. Foremost on their list of grievances was police brutality and the lack of educational opportunities available to them.

Mexican American youth in the cities and towns of the American southwest during that period invented a new term for describing themselves: "Chicano." The word Chicano is loosely based on an Aztec (ancient tribe of Mexican Indians) word, "Meshicano." The name "Chicano" represented Mexican Americans' pride in their cultural heritage.

One man who provided invaluable leadership to the Chicano activists was Rodolfo "Corky" Gonzales. Gonzales, a businessman and political activist, had served as an administrator of government-sponsored social programs in Denver, Colorado, in the early 1960s. In 1965 he founded the Crusade for Justice, a Chicano rights and social service organization

"Writing *I Am Joaquín* was a journey back through history, a painful self-evaluation, a wandering search for my peoples and, most of all, for my own identity."

A dustjacket from an early edition of *I am Joaquín*. *Reproduced by permission of Arte Público Press.*

that worked to end police brutality and discrimination in the public schools.

In 1967 Gonzales wrote the epic poem *I am Joaquín*. The poem traces the history of the ancient Aztecs, Mexicans, and Mexican Americans. Joaquín is a common Mexican name routinely used by police officers to refer to Chicanos whose real names they did not know. The Joaquín in the poem is representative of every Mexican American. *I am Joaquín* is credited with having inspired a spiritual and cultural awakening in a generation of Mexican Americans and is considered the anthem of the Chicano rights movement.

"Writing *I Am Joaquín* was a journey back through history," wrote Gonzales in the introduction to the poem, "a painful self-evaluation, a wandering search for my peoples and, most of all, for my own identity. The totality of all social inequities and injustice had to come to the surface.... *I Am Joaquín* was written as a revelation of myself and of all Chicanos who are Joaquín."

Things to remember while reading the excerpt from *I Am Joaquín*:

- Mexico achieved its independence from Spain in 1821. In 1846 the United States declared war on Mexico. Within two years Mexico had lost the northern half of its territory to the United States.

- The United States-Mexico War came to an end in 1848 with the signing of the Treaty of Guadelupe Hidalgo. Under the treaty, Mexico ceded (gave up) 530,706 square miles of land to the United States in exchange for $15 million. That land has since been carved into the states of California, New Mexico, Arizona, and parts of Colorado, Nevada, and Utah. The 80,000 Mexicans living on that land were declared U.S. citizens and promised the right to retain their property. In the years to come, however, the U.S. failed to honor the treaty. Most of the land belonging to Mexicans in the United States was stolen by prospectors, ranchers, or government agencies.

- During the Mexican Revolution of 1911–14, the dictator of thirty-five years, Porfirio Díaz (1830–1915), was overthrown. Under Díaz's reign, a small number of Mexicans had controlled most of the wealth while the majority of the population had lived in poverty.

- Since the 1880s large numbers of Mexican workers have come to the United States to toil in agricultural fields or at other low-paying and dangerous occupations.

Excerpt from I Am Joaquín

I am Joaquín,
lost in a world of confusion,
caught up in the whirl of a
   ***gringo** society,*
confused by the rules,
scorned by attitudes,
suppressed by manipulation,
and destroyed by modern society.
My fathers
   have lost the economic battle
and won
   the struggle of cultural survival.

And now!
   I must choose
      between
   *the **paradox** of*
victory of the spirit,
despite physical hunger,
      or

Gringo: Mexican word for a person from the United States.

Paradox: Statement that appears to be contradictory, but which may contain a truth.

to exist in the grasp
*of American social **neurosis,***
sterilization of the soul
    and a full stomach.

Yes,
I have come a long way to nowhere,
unwillingly dragged by that
        monstrous, technical,
        industrial giant called
                Progress
*and **Anglo** success....*

I look at myself.
    I watch my brothers.
        I shed tears of sorrow.
            I sow seeds of hate.
I withdraw to the safety within the
circle of life—
            MY OWN PEOPLE.

I owned the land as far as the eye
could see under the crown of Spain,
and I toiled on my earth
and gave my Indian sweat and blood
        for the Spanish master
who ruled with tyranny over man and
beast and all that he could trample.
            But ...
        THE GROUND WAS MINE.
I was both tyrant and slave.

I am Joaquín.
*I rode with **Pancho Villa,***
    crude and warm,
a tornado at full strength,
nourished and inspired
    by the passion and the fire
    of all his earthy people.
*I am **Emiliano Zapata.***
    "This land,
        this earth
            is
                OURS."

Neurosis: Emotional disorder characterized by anxiety and compulsiveness.

Anglo: Person of European descent.

Pancho Villa: 1877–1923; leader of the Mexican Revolution of 1911–14.

Emiliano Zapata: 1877?–1919; leader of the Mexican Revolution of 1911–14.

The villages
   the mountains
     the streams
       belong to **Zapatistas.**
   Our life
     or yours
is the only trade for soft brown earth
and maize.
All of which is our reward,
   a creed that formed a constitution
     for all who dare live free!
"This land is ours ...
   Father, I give it back to you.
     Mexico must be free...."

I stand here looking back,
and now I see
   the present,
and still
   I am the **campesino,**
   I am the fat political **coyote**—
       I,
of the same name,
     Joaquín,
in a country that has wiped out
all my history,
     stifled all my pride,
in a country that has placed a
different weight of indignity upon
     my
       age-
         old
           burdened back.
     Inferiority
is the new load....

The Indian has endured and still
emerged the winner,
  the **Mestizo**
 must yet overcome,
   And the **gachupín**
will just ignore.
  I look at myself

Zapatistas: Mexican independence fighters, followers of Emiliano Zapata.

Campesino: Spanish word for a farmer or farm worker.

Coyote: Spanish word for a person who exploits the suffering or desperation of others for his or her own political or economic gain.

Mestizo: Spanish word meaning a person of mixed Indian and Spanish blood.

Gachupín: Term used by Mexican Indians to describe the Spanish invaders.

Rodolfo "Corky" Gonzales

Rodolfo "Corky" Gonzales was born in Denver, Colorado, in 1929, to a family of migrant farm workers. Gonzales attended public schools in the fall and winter, and spent his summer vacations working alongside his family in the sugar beet fields. After graduating from high school, Gonzales worked in a packing house and as a lumberjack. In the second half of the 1950s he became an owner-operator of a neighborhood bar and began working with the Denver Democratic Party.

Gonzales rapidly ascended the ranks of the Democratic Party. He directed John F. Kennedy's (1917–1963) successful presidential campaign in Colorado in 1960, and from 1964 until 1966 he served as director of Denver's War on Poverty youth programs. (The War on Poverty was a set of social programs intended to provide economic opportunities to the nation's poorest citizens, initiated by Democratic President Lyndon B. Johnson [1908–1973].) While working with the War on Poverty, Gonzales became dismayed by the discrimination he witnessed against Mexican Americans in government programs, as well as the under-representation of Latinos in government agencies. In protest, Gonzales left his job in 1966 and withdrew his membership in the Democratic Party.

In 1965 Gonzales founded the Crusade for Justice, a social-service and

and see part of me
who rejects my father and my mother
and dissolves into the melting pot
   to disappear in shame.
    I sometimes
    sell my brother out
   and reclaim him
for my own when society gives me
   token leadership
     in society's own name.

Here I stand
    before the court of justice,
      guilty
*for all the glory of my **Raza***
     to be sentenced to despair.
Here I stand,

Raza: Spanish word for race. Used in *I Am Joaquín* to mean Mexican people.

Rodolfo "Corky" Gonzales. *Reproduced by permission of the* Denver Post.

political-advocacy organization for Chicanos. The Crusade ran a kindergarten-through-twelfth-grade school, called the Tlatelolco School (after the ancient Aztec city near present-day Mexico City), which offered courses in Mexican history and culture in addition to the standard academic subjects.

Gonzales expressed his aspirations for Chicano political and economic self-determination not only through social activism, but also through literature. Gonzales's most famous work was his epic poem *I Am Joaquín*. He also wrote the poem "Sol, Lágrimas, Sangre" ("Sun, Tears, Blood"), and two plays, *The Revolutionist* and *A Cross for Maclovio*.

poor in money,
arrogant with pride,
    bold with **machismo**,
   rich in courage
     and
    wealthy in spirit and faith.

My knees are caked with mud.
My hands calloused from the hoe.
I have made the Anglo rich,
    yet
equality is but a word—
   the **Treaty of Hidalgo**
has been broken
  and is but another treacherous promise.
My land is lost
    and stolen,

Machismo: Spanish word for masculinity.

Treaty of Hidalgo: Treaty that ended the United States-Mexico War of 1846 to 1848. It transferred more than 530,000 square miles of Mexican land to the United States. The treaty also guaranteed U.S. citizenship to Mexicans living on that land and promised the Mexicans the right to retain their property.

My culture has been raped.
        I lengthen
            the line at the welfare door
and fill the jails with crime.

These then
are the rewards
        this society has
for sons of chiefs
        and kings
        and bloody revolutionists,
who
gave a foreign people
        all their skills and ingenuity
to pave the way with brains and blood
for
those hordes of gold-starved
                            strangers,
who
changed our language
and plagiarized our deeds
            as feats of valor
            of their own.

They frowned upon our way of life
    and took what they could use.
            Our art,
            our literature,
            our music, they ignored—
so they left the real things of value
and grabbed at their own destruction
            by their greed and avarice.
They overlooked that cleansing fountain of
            nature and brotherhood
    which is Joaquín.
        The art of our great señores,
Diego Rivera,
Siqueiros,
Orozco, *is but*
another act of revolution for
        the salvation of mankind.
    Mariachi music, the
        heart and soul

Diego Rivera: 1886–1957; Mexican painter and muralist.

David Alfaro Siqueiros: 1896–1974; Mexican painter and muralist.

Jose Clemente Orozco: 1883–1949; Mexican painter and muralist.

of the people of the earth,
the life of the child,
and the happiness of love.

I am in the eyes of woman,
  sheltered beneath
her shawl of black,
  deep and sorrowful
    eyes
that bear the pain of sons long buried
  or dying,
    dead
on the battlefield or on the barbed wire
  of social strife.

Her rosary she prays and fingers
endlessly
  like the family
working down a row of beets
  to turn around
  and work
  and work.
  There is no end.
Her eyes a mirror of all the warmth
      and all the love for me,
and I am her
and she is me.
  We face life together in sorrow,
  anger, joy, faith and wishful
  thoughts.

I shed the tears of anguish
as I see my children disappear
behind the shroud of mediocrity,
never to look back to remember me.
I am Joaquín.
    I must fight
      and win this struggle
      for my sons, and they
      must know from me
      who I am.
Part of the blood that runs deep in me
could not be vanquished by the **Moors.**
I defeated them after five hundred years,

Moors: People of Arab descent who conquered Spain in the eighth century A.D.

and I endured.
            Part of the blood that is mine
            has labored endlessly four hundred
            years under the heel of lustful
            Europeans.
                    I am still here!

I have endured in the rugged mountains
    of our country.
I have survived the toils and slavery
    of the fields.
                    I have existed
in the **barrios** of the city
in the suburbs of bigotry
in the mines of social snobbery
in the prisons of dejection
in the muck of exploitation
and
in the fierce heat of racial hatred.

And now the trumpet sounds,
the music of the people stirs the
                    revolution.
Like a sleeping giant it slowly
rears its head
to the sound of
                    tramping feet
                    clamoring voices
                    mariachi strains
                fiery tequila explosions
            the smell of **chile verde** and
            soft brown eyes of expectation for a
                                better life.

And in all the fertile farmlands,
                            the barren plains,
the mountain villages,
smoke-smeared cities,
            we start to MOVE.

    La Raza!
Méjicano!
        Español!
            Latino!

Barrios: Spanish word for neighborhoods of Spanish-speaking people.

Chile verde: Spanish words for green chili.

Méjicano: Mexican (adjective) or a Mexican person.

Español: Spanish (adjective), Spanish language, or a Spaniard.

Latino: Person living in the United States who was born in, or whose descendants were born in, a Spanish-speaking country (synonymous with Hispano and Hispanic).

> *Hispano!*
>   *Chicano!*
> *or whatever I call myself,*
>   *I look the same*
>   *I feel the same*
>   *I cry*
>   *and*
>   *sing the same.*
>
> *I am the masses of my people and*
> *I refuse to be absorbed.*
>   *I am Joaquín.*
> *The odds are great*
> *but my spirit is strong,*
>   *my faith unbreakable,*
>   *my blood is pure.*
> *I am **Aztec** prince and Christian Christ.*
>   *I SHALL ENDURE!*
>   *I WILL ENDURE!*

(Gonzales, pp. 6–12, 18–19, 34–37, 51–53, 64–71, 77–79, 82, 86, 93, 96–100)

Hispano: Person living in the United States who was born in, or whose descendants were born in, a Spanish-speaking country (synonymous with Hispanic and Latino).

Chicano: Term used by politically active Mexican Americans to describe themselves.

Aztec: Ancient tribe of Indians who lived in what is present-day southern Mexico.

What happened next...

In March 1969 hundreds of Denver high school students walked out of their classes. Like so many uprisings by Chicano students throughout the Southwest, the Denver student protest was in response to discriminatory practices in the schools. Among the students' many grievances were the schools' ban on Spanish speaking and school counselors' practice of directing Chicano students into vocational classes while advising white students to take college preparatory classes.

A few days after the Denver student walk-out, the Crusade for Justice sponsored a five-day gathering called the National Chicano Youth Liberation Conference. This conference drew the participation of more than 1,500 young Chicanos from all over the United States. Attendees went to work-

Attendees in the Lincoln Memorial reflecting pool at the 1968 Poor Peoples' March on Washington, D.C. At the invitation of Martin Luther King Jr., Gonzales cochaired the Mexican American contingent of the march. *Reproduced by permission of AP/Wide World Photos.*

shops on civil rights and cultural topics, such as Mexican poetry, literature, song, dance, and theater. They also grappled with defining their roles, as Chicanos, within the context of American society.

Chicano activists formed their own political party in late 1969, called the La Raza Unida (pronounced la RAHssa oonEEDa; the name means "The People United"). Gonzales and other La Raza activists had come to the conclusion that neither the Democratic Party nor the Republican Party could be counted on to act in the interest of Chicanos. The platform of the La Raza Unida Party called for bilingual education, the regulation of public utilities (to prevent gas and electricity companies from hitting consumers with sharp price increases), farm subsidies, and a tax structure that favored low-income people.

In September 1972 Gonzales organized the first national convention of La Raza Unida in El Paso, Texas. More than 3,000 delegates came to the convention, representing the sixteen states in which the party had chapters. In 1972 and 1973 La Raza candidates were elected to local positions throughout the Southwest. The party's influence, however, was short-lived. By 1974 Crystal City was the only locality in which La Raza Unida members held office.

Did you know...

- *I am Joaquín* was published in both Spanish and in English. It was recited at numerous demonstrations, performed by theater troupes, and made into a film.

- While a high school student, Gonzales won the Golden Gloves amateur boxing title. At age eighteen Gonzales became a professional boxer. He retired from boxing in 1955, after having won sixty-five of his seventy-five matches.

- At the invitation of Martin Luther King Jr. (1929–1968), Gonzales co-chaired the Mexican American contingent of the Poor People's March. The Poor People's March, conceived of by King shortly before his death, was a gathering in Washington, D.C., of thousands of poor people of all races, from all parts of the country. Participants set up a tent city near the Capitol building and lobbied legislators for programs that would expand economic opportunity.

Sources

Books

Gonzales, Rodolfo. *I Am Joaquín/Yo Soy Joaquín*. New York: Bantam Books, 1972.

Martinez, Elizabeth Sutherland, and Enriqueta Longeaux y Vásquez. *Viva la Raza!: The Struggle of the Mexican-American People*. Garden City, NY: Doubleday and Company, Inc., 1974.

Nagel, Rob, and Sharon Rose, eds. *Hispanic American Biography*, Vol. 1. Detroit: U•X•L, 1995, pp. 94–97.

Rosales, F. Arturo. *Chicano! The History of the Mexican American Civil Rights Movement*. Houston, TX: Arte Público Press, 1997.

Sigler, Jay A., ed. *Civil Rights in America: 1500 to the Present*. Detroit: Gale, Inc., 1998.

Steiner, Stan. *La Raza: The Mexican-Americans*. New York: Harper and Row, 1969.

Other

Chicano! The History of the Mexican American Civil Rights Movement (video-cassette; four episodes). Los Angeles: NLCC Educational Media, 1996.

Vernon Bellecourt

"Birth of AIM"

**Excerpt reprinted in *Native American Testimony: A Chronicle of Indian-White Relations from Prophecy to the Present, 1492–1992*
Published in 1991**

The American Indian Movement (AIM) was the best-known and most militant organization to emerge from the "Red Power" movement. The Red Power movement was a sustained series of protest activities by Native Americans in the 1960s and 1970s. The Indian activists were responding to the injustices inflicted on the Indian people by U.S. government policies, particularly the policies of termination (the ending of treaty rights) and relocation (the resettlement of Indians from reservations to cities).

The activists were also striving to improve the horrible living conditions of Indians on reservations and in cities. In the early 1960s life expectancy of American Indians was only forty years on average, and the infant mortality rate of Indians was ten times that of the national average. Tens of thousands of Indian families lived in dilapidated shacks or in broken-down vehicles. Indian adolescents led the nation in numbers of suicides per capita.

Like other groups in the Red Power movement, AIM fought for greater economic opportunities for Indians, respect for Indian human rights, the return of tribal lands, and the

"We have the spirituality, yet we are warriors. We'll stand up and fight for our people."

Vernon Bellecourt is a spokesperson for the National Coalition on Racism in Sports and Media, an organization working to end the use of Indian mascots and nicknames by sports teams. *Reproduced by permission of Corbis-Bettmann.*

enforcement of government treaties. AIM patterned itself on the Black Panthers, an African American self-defense and community improvement organization founded in Oakland, California, in 1966. AIM was famous for using confrontational, and sometimes violent, tactics to shake up what the organization considered an unresponsive and inhumane political system.

As Vernon Bellecourt describes in "Birth of AIM," the original mission of AIM was to stop police brutality against Native Americans in Minneapolis (like other people of color, Indians were frequently harassed and beaten by white police officers). AIM's mission rapidly expanded to cover a range of human rights and land issues. By the end of the 1960s AIM chapters had been set up across the United States in cities with sizable Indian populations.

Things to remember while reading "Birth of AIM":

- Vernon Bellecourt's brother, Clyde Bellecourt, was among the founders of AIM in 1968. Vernon joined the leadership of the organization soon after it was formed. Today Vernon is a spokesperson for the National Coalition on Racism in Sports and Media, an organization working to end the use of Indian mascots and nicknames by sports teams.

- The original name selected for the American Indian Movement was "Concerned Indian Americans." This name was ultimately rejected because its initials, CIA, were identical to the U.S. government intelligence-gathering organization, the Central Intelligence Agency.

- One of the first large-scale protest activities in which AIM members participated was the takeover of Alcatraz Island (the former penal colony in San Francisco Bay). The leaders of the occupation—which lasted from November 1969 until June 1971—demanded that the island, which had once been populated by Indians, be given back to Indians.

"Birth of AIM"

*I had seven brothers and sisters. First I went to a public school, and it became a **parochial school** open to all the kids in the community. I went there until the eighth grade, to junior high school for one year and quit. Couldn't handle the racist attitudes, the abuse I got, so I dropped out in the ninth grade....*

*I lived on the **reservation** until I was fifteen. I recognized despair was setting in, because I was caught up in poverty in a large family with never quite enough food on the table. Leaving the reservation and going into the city was the start of becoming Anglo-oriented....*

When I was about twenty years old, I was an armed robber, sort of a Robin Hood type. It was my way of getting back at the system for ripping us off. This was in Minnesota. I ended up in prison doing a forty-year sentence. They have what they call a youth program; if you don't commit any more crimes after they release you, they wipe your record clean. But I was bitter. When they let me out I did it again, and I got caught. Then I had forty years to do plus another five. I did three and a half years, finally won a discharge on the forty-year sentence and got paroled on the five. Then I knew I could never do that again—not especially because I thought it was wrong, but because I didn't want to go to jail anymore. In prison they taught me how to be a barber, and after I came out, I ended up owning a beauty salon. From that I went into the import business, gift items and such....

*My brother Clyde was doing a tremendous amount of time in Stillwater State Prison in Minnesota, and he just gave up in despair and wouldn't eat. He went on a hunger strike and was going to stay on it until he died. He met a young **Ojibwa** brother who was from a medicine family, a family of spiritual leaders, and this young man was also a spiritual leader.*

*This young **medicine man**, Eddie Benton, was sort of a **trusty**, and he'd come by my brother's cell and try to talk to him and ask him*

Parochial school: School run by a religious organization.

Reservation: Tract of land set aside by the U.S. government for use by an Indian tribe.

Ojibwa: Large tribe of North American Indians, occupying land around Lake Superior in Canada and the United States. Also called Ojibway or Chippewa.

Medicine man: American Indian spiritual leader and healer.

Trusty: In this case, a jailed person who enjoys special privileges because she/he is reliable or trustworthy.

to eat. But Clyde wouldn't eat. Finally Eddie started throwing candy bars in there, but they just piled up, and my brother wouldn't touch them. Then one day he started quoting literature, telling about the Ojibwas and our proud heritage. And finally one day, I guess just out of boredom, my brother picked up a piece of this literature and started reading about us. And he finally recognized he wasn't the dirty Indian he'd been told he was by White students at school....

So anyway, Clyde started reading this literature, and it brought him back to life and gave him renewed strength and dignity. He started eating and started to get involved. He and Eddie Benton started an Indian awareness program in the prison and were instrumental in keeping our young Indian men out of jail once they got out....

When Clyde got out of prison early in 1968, he went to work for a power company. He had one of the first organizational meetings, in mid-1968, with a group of people in Minneapolis, in the Indian ghetto community. Everything was deteriorating rather than getting better. There were police harassment and brutality, because of a complete breakdown of police-community relations.

At the first meeting Clyde attended, they voted him the national director. There were twenty-seven or twenty-eight other Indian organizations in the Minneapolis community. Most of them were related to various churches—missionary work in disguise. For the most part, the boards of these organizations were White dominated. White do-gooders as consultants and advisers controlled them.

So the first AIM was formed in Minneapolis, as a non-profit corporation with an all-Indian board and staff. They were going to call the organization The Concerned Indian Americans, CIA. They couldn't use that! So a couple of older, respected women said, "Well, you keep saying that you aim *to do this, you* aim *to do that. Why don't you call it AIM, the American Indian Movement?" That's how we got our name....*

I watched what they were doing, and I could see the pride in these young men and women. A new dignity, a new awareness, a new power, a new strength. Then I looked at myself, I was making money and living in White suburbia.... So I went up to Minnesota, and for about a week I visited with my brother and other people in the movement—Russell Means, Dennis Banks and some of the founders. Finally I got so involved I started letting my hair grow long, and I stopped wearing a tie and started to sort of de-program myself, to become just

"Keep Your Presents"

In the mid-1800s, Curly Chief was a leader of one of the four tribes that comprised the Pawnee Confederation. The Pawnees were hunters and farmers living near the Platte River in Nebraska. In 1849, as white settlers headed to California at the height of the gold rush, they passed through the Pawnee land. The whites spread smallpox and cholera—diseases caused the deaths of one-quarter of the Pawnee people. The Pawnees were relocated to northern Oklahoma in 1875.

In the following undated essay titled "Keep Your Presents", Curly Chief recalls an early encounter between Indians and white men:

I heard that long ago there was a time when there were no people in this country except Indians. After that, the people began to hear of men that had white skins; they had been seen far to the east. Before I was born, they came out to our country and visited us. The man who came was from the Government. He wanted to make a treaty with us, and to give us presents, blankets and guns, flint and steel, and knives.

The Head Chief told him that we needed none of these things. He said, "We have our buffalo and our corn. These things the Ruler gave to us, and they are all that we need. See this robe. This keeps me warm in winter. I need no blanket."

The white men had with them some cattle, and the Pawnee Chief said, "Lead out a heifer here on the prairie." They led her out, and the Chief, stepping up to her, shot her through behind the shoulder with his arrow, and she fell down and died. Then the Chief said, "Will not my arrow kill? I do not need your guns." Then he took his stone knife and skinned the heifer, and cut off a piece of fat meat. When he had done this, he said, "Why should I take your knives? The Ruler has given me something to cut with."

Then taking the fire sticks, he kindled a fire to roast the meat, and while it was cooking, he spoke again and said, "You see, my brother, that the Ruler has given us all that we need; the buffalo for food and clothing; the corn to eat with our dried meat; bows, arrows, knives and hoes; all the implements which we need for killing meat, or for cultivating the ground. Now go back to the country from whence you came. We do not want your presents, and we do not want you to come into our country.

Originally printed in Pawnee Hero Stories and Folk Tales, *edited by George Grinnell. New York, 1889; reprinted in* Native American Testimony: A Chronicle of Indian-White Relations from Prophecy to the Present, 1492–1992, *edited by Peter Nabokov. New York: Viking, 1991.*

a simple person, a simple man. More humble. I saw in that something I could identify with....

When AIM was forming, one of the first things they zeroed in on was police-community relations. Young men and women in the com-

munity formed the AIM patrol. They had red jackets with thunderbird emblems on the backs.

Sometimes they appointed somebody to the Patrol who had a bad drinking problem; one of the qualifications, of course, was being sober. So it was really an alcoholic rehabilitation program at the same time....

They got a small grant from the Urban League of Minneapolis to put two-way radios in their cars and to get tape recorders and cameras. They would listen to the police calls, and when they heard there was going to be an arrest or that police were being dispatched to a certain community or bar, they'd show up with cameras and take pictures of the police using more than normal restraint on the people.

They got evidence of beatings and of ripping people around with handcuffs too tight, ripping their wrists. It was very vicious. This sometimes becomes a way of life for the police. They just fall into it. They think that's the way Indians have to be treated. So AIM would show up and have attorneys ready. Often they would beat the police back to the station. They would have a bondsman there, and they'd start filing law suits against the police department....

Members recognized there was something missing from the movement. They heard about a medicine man in South Dakota, a holy man, a spirit leader. Now, the spirituality of Indian people has always been strong and has remained intact in some areas of South Dakota. They heard about Leonard Crow Dog, a medicine man who was maybe twenty-five. They were curious, and they went to visit him and his dad.... Well, they went there for advice, and one of the first questions they asked was, "What is an Indian?" They wanted to redefine what they were. And they were told that to be an Indian is to be spiritual.... We have the spirituality, yet we are warriors. We'll stand up and fight for our people. We haven't had that for many years. The warrior class of this century is bound by the bond of the drum.... That circle around the drum brings us together. We can have two or three hundred people around that drum, all from different tribes, all singing the same song. We put out a bumper sticker, "AIM for **Sovereignty.**" Most of our people didn't even know what the word meant. Now they know.

Vernon Bellecourt, Chippewa. (Nabokov, pp. 372–76)

Sovereignty: State of being independent and self-governed.

What happened next...

Between the years 1969 and 1979, AIM either initiated or supported numerous protest actions around the United States. For example, in September 1970 an AIM delegation—led by activists Russell Means, John Trudell, and Lee Brightman—demonstrated at Mount Rushmore National Park in the Black Hills of South Dakota. Some fifty AIM members climbed to the top of the four presidential heads chiseled into the rocky hillside. The group demanded that all lands in South Dakota west of the Missouri River, including Mount Rushmore and the rest of the Black Hills, be returned to the Sioux in accordance with the Treaty of Fort Laramie. (Under the terms of the 1868 Treaty of Fort Laramie, the U.S. government promised to return to the Sioux all lands in South Dakota west of the Missouri River, including Mount Rushmore and the rest of the Black Hills.)

Two months later AIM sponsored a Thanksgiving Day protest near the original Plymouth Colony in Massachusetts. The purpose of the demonstration was to call attention to the massacre of Wampanoag Indians by the Pilgrims which, according to AIM, was the true reason for the first Thanksgiving celebration. The Indian protesters disrupted the feast underway in the Plimoth Plantation (a living-history museum of seventeenth-century Plymouth) village hall, then took over a ship docked in the harbor that was a replica of the *Mayflower* (the ship on which the original Pilgrims came to America). After dark, some members of the AIM group scaled the protective fence around the Plymouth Rock monument and covered the rock with red paint. The paint symbolized the spilled blood of the Wampanoag Indians.

In the fall of 1972 AIM members from around the United States held a Trail of Broken Treaties protest in Washington, D.C. After presenting the Bureau of Indian Affairs (BIA) with a list of demands, including the restoration of tribes' treaty-making status, the return of stolen Indian lands, and the revocation of state government authority over Indian affairs, the demonstrators took over the building. They left the building six days later, after having destroyed BIA property, and smuggled out files containing evidence of BIA corruption.

In late February 1973 AIM initiated a ten-week-long takeover of the village of Wounded Knee in the Pine Ridge

Reservation in South Dakota. (Wounded Knee was significant because it was the site of the 1890 massacre of between 150 and 370 Native American men, women, and children by U.S. military forces.) Together with hundreds of Pine Ridge Reservation residents, AIM activists protested the corrupt practices of tribal chairman Richard Wilson and the brutality of his police force, the Guardians of the Oglala Nation (commonly referred to as the "GOON squad").

Throughout the occupation, Wounded Knee was encircled by hundreds of FBI agents, U.S. marshals, and members of tribal and local police forces. The law enforcement officers were equipped with firearms, armored personnel carriers, grenade launchers, 600 cases of tear gas, helicopters, and Phantom jets. Negotiations produced an end to the siege on May 8. While the takeover did not succeed in removing Wilson from government, it did thrust the problems confronting Native Americans into the spotlight of the national media.

AIM remained at the fore of the Red Power movement through the end of the 1970s. After that time, AIM became weakened by internal problems and was slowed in its mission by a general conservative trend in American politics and society. While AIM still exists today, its membership and influence have declined in the 1980s and 1990s.

Did you know...

- AIM was infiltrated, and its members harassed, by the Federal Bureau of Investigation (FBI) under the guise of the agency's Counter-Intelligence Program (COINTELPRO). The stated purpose of COINTELPRO was to combat domestic terrorism. In reality, COINTELPRO was used to weaken the anti-Vietnam War and civil rights movements, along with the Black Panther Party, AIM, and other militant organizations of people of color. By the end of the 1970s the FBI had succeeded in greatly diminishing AIM's effectiveness.

- During the two years following the siege of Wounded Knee, sixty-nine AIM members were gunned down or died under mysterious circumstances on the Pine Ridge Reservation. Most of the deaths came at the hands of Dick Wilson's GOON squads.

Sources

Books

Deloria, Vine, Jr. *Custer Died for Your Sins: An Indian Manifesto.* New York: Macmillan, 1969.

Deloria, Vine, Jr., and Clifford M. Lytle. *The Nations Within: The Past and Future of American Indian Sovereignty.* New York: Pantheon Books, 1984.

Johansen, Bruce E., and Donald A. Grinde, Jr. *The Encyclopedia of Native American Biography: Six Hundred Life Stories of Important People from Powhatan to Wilma Mankiller.* New York: Da Capo Press, 1998.

Josephy, Alvin M., Jr., ed. *Red Power: The American Indians' Fight for Freedom.* New York: McGraw-Hill Book Company, 1971.

Means, Russell, and Marvin J. Wolf. *Where White Men Fear to Tread: The Autobiography of Russell Means.* New York: St. Martin's Press, 1995.

Nabokov, Peter, ed. *American Indian Testimony: A Chronicle of Indian-White Relations from Prophecy to the Present, 1492–1992.* New York: Viking, 1991.

Smith, Paul Chaat, and Robert Allen Warrior. *Like A Hurricane: The Indian Movement from Alcatraz to Wounded Knee.* New York: The New Press, 1995.

Other

Apted, Michael, director. *Incident at Oglala: The Leonard Peltier Story* (documentary). Miramax, 1992.

Apted, Michael, director. *Thunderheart.* Columbia, 1992.

Commission on Wartime Relocation and Internment of Civilians

Personal Justice Denied

**Excerpt from the commission's report
Originally published in 1983**

Ever since their arrival in the United States in the latter half of the nineteenth century, Japanese immigrants to the United States and their offspring faced discrimination. The main reason for the unfriendly reception was that white workers viewed Japanese workers as unwanted competition. Anti-immigrant politicians, spurred on by nativist organizations, enacted a series of discriminatory laws. The first of these laws was the Naturalization Act of 1870, which prevented Japanese immigrants (and other Asians) from becoming naturalized American citizens. The Immigration Act of 1924 put an end to virtually all Japanese immigration to the United States. The Alien Land Act, in effect from 1913 to 1948, forbade Japanese nationals from owning land in California (the state in which the majority of Japanese immigrants and their families lived).

Throughout the Great Depression (the worst economic crisis ever to hit the United States, lasting from 1929 and to 1939) anti-Japanese sentiment escalated. Along with other immigrants and people of color, Japanese Americans were blamed for the economic collapse. Anti-Japanese sentiment reached a frenzied pitch on December 7, 1941, when Japan

"I lost my identity....
[The] WRA gave me an
I. D. number. That was
my identification. I lost
my privacy and dignity."

*Betty Matsuo, San Francisco,
August 11, 1981*

On February 19, 1942, President Franklin D. Roosevelt signed Executive Order 9066, which authorized the mass removal of Japanese Americans from the West Coast.
Reproduced by permission of the Franklin D. Roosevelt Library.

bombed the naval station at Pearl Harbor, Hawaii (this act drew the United States into active participation in World War II, 1939–45).

White Americans exacted revenge for the bombing on Japanese Americans. People of Japanese ancestry were beaten on the streets; Japanese American parents considered it too dangerous to send their children to school. Individuals, civic organizations, and local governments accused all Japanese Americans of being enemy sympathizers and called for mass arrests.

Immediately after the bombing, a series of restrictions and punitive measures were placed on Japanese Americans. Several hundred Japanese nationals were arrested. Japanese Americans were fired by public and private employers, forced to observe a curfew, and fingerprinted. U.S. servicemen of Japanese descent were discharged from the military and Japanese-language newspapers were banned.

On February 19, 1942, President Franklin Delano Roosevelt signed Executive Order 9066, thereby authorizing the mass removal of Japanese Americans from the West Coast. Roosevelt's directive led to the eventual internment of 120,000 Japanese Americans in camps from 1942 through 1945 (in some cases through March 1946).

In early 1942 Japanese Americans began receiving their evacuation orders. The orders typically gave a person less than seven days to report to a relocation processing (or assembly) center. There were twenty relocation processing centers along the West Coast, most of them set up in fairgrounds, racetracks, abandoned military facilities, migrant work camps, and stockyards. The evacuees were only allowed to bring those possessions they could carry.

After spending, on average, 100 days at a relocation processing center, the prisoners were transported to one of ten relocation camps. The camps were located in the inland portion of the western United States; many of them were in dry, windy, desolate regions that had bitterly cold winters.

In 1981, thirty-five years after the last camp was closed, Congress created the Commission on Wartime Relocation and Internment of Civilians. The purpose of the commission was to assess the damage done to Japanese American citizens and Japanese resident aliens by their internment during World War II. The Commission held twenty days of public hearings—most of them on the West Coast between July and December 1981—at which testimony was presented by more than 750 witnesses. Those testifying included former detainees, former government officials, and researchers who had studied the internment.

On June 23, 1983, the Commission delivered its report to Congress, entitled *Personal Justice Denied*. The report was a scathing indictment of the U.S. government's treatment of Japanese Americans during World War II. The Commission determined that there had been no military necessity for the incarceration of the Japanese Americans. It concluded that the decision to imprison Japanese Americans had been driven by war hysteria, racial prejudice, and a lack of political leadership.

The Commission recommended that Congress pass a resolution apologizing for the grave injustice done to Japanese Americans, offer reparations in the amount of $20,000 to each of the 60,000 prison camp survivors and erase the records of persons of Japanese ancestry convicted of violating the West Coast curfew in 1942.

Things to remember while reading excerpts from *Personal Justice Denied*:

- Upon receiving their evacuation orders, Japanese Americans were left with little choice but to sell their property. In many cases, driven by desperation, they sold their property for a mere fraction of the property's value. Non-Japanese individuals took advantage of the Japanese Americans' misfortune, buying up cars, furniture, homes, and businesses at rock-bottom prices.

- Regardless of the abuse and humiliation to which they were subjected, Japanese American detainees were expected to demonstrate their loyalty to the United States. At schools established in the camps, children had to start each day by saluting the American flag and singing "My Country 'tis of Thee."

On February 8, 1943, all camp occupants over the age of seventeen were forced to answer a loyalty questionnaire. One of the questions was: "Will you swear unqualified allegiance to the United States of America and faithfully defend the United States from any or all attack by foreign or domestic sources, and forswear any form of allegiance or obedience to the Japanese emperor, or any other foreign government, power or organization?"

Detainees who responded negatively to that question (which many did, in protest of their treatment) were sent to a segregation facility—Tule Lake camp in California. In addition to individuals who refused to swear loyalty to the United States, Tule Lake housed men who had refused the draft and people who were accused of being agents of Japan.

- The worst conditions in any camp were found in the confinement area, known as the "bull pen," at Tule Lake. Individuals in any of the ten relocation camps who protested their confinement were sent to the Tule Lake bull pen.

Excerpts from Personal Justice Denied

Our house was in from Garden Grove Boulevard about 200 yards on a dirt driveway and on the day before the posted evacuation date, there was a line up of cars in our driveway extending about another 200 yards in both directions along Garden Grove Boulevard, waiting their turn to come to our house....

—*Hiroshi Kamei, Los Angeles, August 6, 1981*

Swarms of people came daily to our home to see what they could buy. A grand piano for $50, pieces of furniture, $50.... One man offered $500 for the house.

—Henry Yoshitake, Montebello, CA, unsolicited testimony

It is difficult to describe the feeling of despair and humiliation experienced by all of us as we watched the Caucasians coming to look over our possessions and offering such nominal amounts knowing we had no recourse but to accept whatever they were offering because we did not know what the future held for us.

—Yasuko Ito, San Francisco, August 13, 1981

People who were like vultures swooped down on us going through our belongings offering us a fraction of their value. When we complained to them of the low price they would respond by saying, "you can't take it with you so take it or leave it."

—Roy Abbey, San Francisco, unsolicited testimony

On May 16, 1942, my mother, two sisters, niece, nephew, and I left ... by train. Father joined us later. Brother left earlier by bus. We took whatever we could carry. So much we left behind, but the most valuable thing I lost was my freedom.

—Teru Watanabe, Los Angeles, August 6, 1981

*I lost my identity. At that time, I didn't even have a Social Security number, but the WRA [**War Relocation Authority**] gave me an I.D. number. That was my identification. I lost my privacy and my dignity.*

—Betty Matsuo, San Francisco, August 11, 1981

*At the entrance [to the Tanforan **assembly center**] ... stood two lines of troops with rifles and fixed bayonets pointed at the evacuees as they walked between the soldiers to the prison compound. Overwhelmed with bitterness and blind rage, I screamed every obscenity I knew at the armed guards daring them to shoot at me.*

—William Kochiyama, New York, November 23, 1981

On May 16, 1942 at 9:30 a.m., we departed ... for an unknown destination. To this day, I can remember vividly the plight of the elderly, some on stretchers, orphans herded onto the train by caretakers, and especially a young couple with four pre-school children. The mother had two frightened toddlers hanging on to her coat. In her arms, she carried two crying babies. The father had diapers and other baby paraphernalia strapped to his back. In his hands he strug-

War Relocation Authority: Federal agency charged with overseeing the welfare of evacuated citizens.

Assembly center: Hastily erected processing center to which Japanese Americans reported after receiving their evacuation orders. There were twenty relocation processing centers on the West Coast, most of them set up in fairgrounds, racetracks, abandoned military facilities, migrant work camps, and stockyards. Detainees spent at average of 100 days at an assembly center before being assigned to a relocation center or camp.

gled with duffel bag and suitcase. The shades were drawn on the train for our entire trip. Military police patrolled the aisles.

—Grace Nakamura, Los Angeles, August 6, 1981

At Parker, Arizona, we were transferred to buses. With baggage and carryalls hanging from my arm, I was contemplating what I could leave behind, since my husband was not allowed to come to my aid. A soldier said, 'Let me help you, put your arm out.' He proceeded to pile everything on my arm. And to my horror, he placed my two-month-old baby on top of the stack. He then pushed me with the butt of the gun and told me to get off the train, knowing when I stepped off the train my baby would fall to the ground. I refused. But he kept prodding and ordering me to move. I will always be thankful [that] a lieutenant checking the cars came upon us. He took the baby down, gave her to me, and then ordered the soldier to carry all our belongings to the bus and see that I was seated and then report back to him.

—Shizuko S. Tokushige, San Francisco, August 12, 1981

*When we first arrived at Minidoka [**relocation center** in Idaho], everyone was forced to use outhouses since the sewer system had not been built. For about a year, the residents had to brave the cold and the stench of these accommodations.*

—Shuzo C. Kato, Seattle, September 9, 1981

The most tragic, as well as traumatic, event that happened during my stay in Tule Lake that still remains with me is the questionnaire with the loyalty oath that was required of all of us to answer. I have never even mentioned this to my children. This, as you may know, was a controversial document that affected each of us 17 years of age or older, in one way or another. We were forced into concentration camps by the government, and then we were being forced into taking a loyalty oath. Furthermore, at this point there was no indication as to what the consequences would be for refusing. We had area block meetings on the issue.... We voted, at that time, as a block, not to sign the loyalty oath.

—Frank Kageta, San Francisco, August 13, 1981

Not only had our government disregarded our citizenship [and] put us behind barbed wire, but now was asking these same citizens to foreswear [sic] allegiance to the Emperor of Japan and to swear allegiance to the United States as if at one time all of us had sworn allegiance to the Japanese Emperor.

—Ben Takeshita, San Francisco, August 11, 1981

Relocation center (camp):
Also called an internment camp, this was a facility that housed some 10,000 Japanese Americans for up to four years. There were ten relocation camps, all located in the inland portion of the western United States.

Our block was located on the southwest corner of the [Tule Lake] camp grounds. The double barbed wire fence was just beyond the next barrack from our compartment. A guard tower with uniformed men and weapons were in view at all times. Search lights were beamed onto the camp grounds at night. Uniformed men with weapons driving around in jeeps was a common sight. As a result of this experience, I used to be afraid of any white male adult for a very long time.

Demonstrations in protest of one thing or other were frequent. We very often locked ourselves in our room to avoid participating in these demonstrations. Physical violence and verbal abuses were common at these demonstrations where feelings ran high. And whenever a large demonstration took place, we could always expect the camp authorities to send out soldiers to search our rooms for **contraband.** *These searches were very thorough and everything was ransacked.*

Life in Tule Lake Segregation Camp for children was not very pleasant. There was very little to do for entertainment. Toys were

Japanese American internees at the Santa Anita Assembly Center in California. *Reproduced by permission of the National Archive and Records Administration.*

Contraband: Any illegal item. In the case of Japanese Americans during World War II, contraband items included weapons, cameras, radio transmitters, and anything else that could be used to conduct acts of espionage.

scarce. We often played hopscotch using the coal pieces from the pile in front of the bathroom area.

—Taeko Sakai Okamura, San Francisco, August 13, 1981

Prisoners in the 'bull pen' were housed outdoors in tents without heat and with no protection against the bitter cold. The bunks were placed directly on the cold ground, and the prisoners had only one or two blankets and no extra clothing to ward off the winter chill. And, for the first time in our lives, those of us confined to the 'bull pen' experienced a life and death struggle for survival, the unbearable pain from our unattended and infected wounds, and the penetrating December cold of Tule Lake, a God Forsaken concentration camp lying near the Oregon border, and I shall never forget that horrible experience.

—Tokio Yamane, unsolicited testimony (location and date not given)

(Commission on Wartime Relocation and Internment of Civilians, pp. 132, 135, 136, 151, 160, 194–95, 247, 248–49)

What happened next...

On December 17, 1944, the army ordered the release of all Japanese Americans from detention. Between January 2, 1945, and September 2, 1945 (the date the U.S. proclaimed victory over Japan), the camps were gradually vacated. The last camp to close, on March 20, 1946, was Tule Lake.

Each detainee, upon release, received $25 and a train ticket to their city of prior residence. Most Japanese Americans had no homes or jobs to return to, since they had sold all their possessions before arriving at the detention centers. Those who attempted to resettle on the West Coast were greeted with hostility, both from their neighbors and from newly formed anti-Japanese citizens' groups.

After their years of detention, most Japanese Americans had no property or savings. They found it exceedingly difficult to find housing or jobs or to reestablish businesses. Some 8,000 Japanese Americans chose to leave the United States.

Immediately after World War II, Japanese Americans began seeking monetary reimbursement from the government for the $400 million they lost by underselling or abandoning their property. They also sought an apology for their unlawful imprisonment.

The first action taken by Congress to compensate survivors for their losses was the passage of the Evacuation Claims Act of 1948. Under the terms of that legislation, Congress appropriated $38 million to compensate Japanese Americans for their financial losses. Former detainees were given 18 months in which to file claims, in order to recover their money. Many Japanese Americans, however, could not file claims because their financial records had been lost or destroyed during their internment. As of June 30, 1954, about $23 million had been paid out to settle 19,750 claims. Many claimants died before receiving their money.

In 1988, acting on recommendations of the Commission on Wartime Relocation and Internment of Civilians, Congress passed the Civil Liberties Act. That legislation authorized the payment of $20,000 to each survivor of the internment camps and contained an apology from Congress to Japanese Americans who had been held in the camps. The first nine checks were issued to the oldest former detainees in October 1990. The final payments were made in 1994.

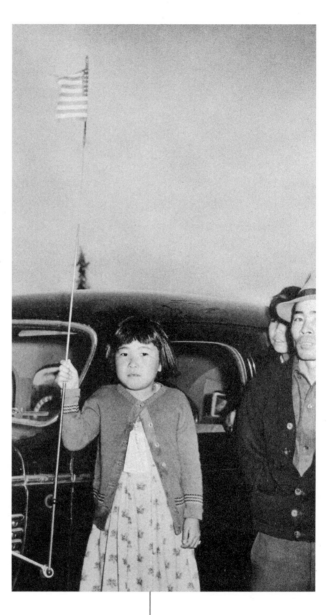

A young girl at an internment camp.
Reproduced by permission of the Library of Congress.

Did you know...

- Several Japanese Americans were killed by armed guards during the four years the internment camps were in operation. Among the fatalities were two seriously ill detainees at the Lordsburg camp in New Mexico; a 63-year-old man who wandered close to the fence and was shot at the Topaz camp in Utah; and a mentally ill detainee at the Gila River, Arizona camp.

• There is widespread speculation that the Japanese Americans were interned one year longer than military officials deemed necessary because of the political aspirations of President Franklin D. Roosevelt. In the spring of 1943 Secretary of War Henry L. Stimson, Assistant Secretary of War John J. McCloy, and General George C. Marshall recommended to the president that the detainees be released, based on the detainees' overwhelmingly positive responses to loyalty questionnaires. Roosevelt, however, knew that the imprisonment of Japanese Americans was wildly popular among the American citizenry and believed that continued detention would aid his chances of reelection in 1944. Roosevelt ordered the military officials to table the matter until after the presidential election.

• The Commission on Wartime Relocation and Internment of Civilians concluded that the internment of Japanese Americans had no military justification. "All this [the internment of 120,000 Japanese Americans] was done," wrote the Commission in *Personal Justice Denied,* "despite the fact that not a single documented act of espionage, sabotage or fifth column activity was committed by an American citizen of Japanese ancestry or by a resident Japanese alien on the West Coast."

Sources

Books

Baron, Deborah G., and Susan B. Gall, eds. *Asian American Chronology.* Detroit: U•X•L, 1996.

Chan, Sucheng. *Asian Americans: An Interpretive History.* Boston: Twayne Publishers, 1991.

Commission on Wartime Relocation and Internment of Civilians. *Personal Justice Denied.* Washington, D.C.: Civil Liberties Public Education Fund, 1983.

Daniels, Roger. *Asian America: Chinese and Japanese in the United States since 1850.* Seattle: University of Washington Press, 1988.

Hatamiya, Leslie T. *Righting a Wrong: Japanese Americans and the Passage of the Civil Liberties Act.* Stanford, California: Stanford University Press, 1993.

Natividad, Irene, and Susan B. Gall, eds. *Asian American Almanac.* Detroit: U•X•L, 1996.

Sigler, Jay A., ed. *Civil Rights in America: 1500 to the Present.* Detroit: Gale, 1998.

Weglyn, Michi. *Years of Infamy: The Untold Story of America's Concentration Camps.* New York: William Morrow and Company, Inc., 1976.

National American Woman Suffrage Association

"Women Should Have the Right to Vote"

Originally published in 1904 as "Declaration of Principles"
Excerpt from *Feminism: Opposing Viewpoints*
Published in 1995

In 1904 the National American Woman Suffrage Association outlined its argument for women's suffrage (the right to vote in public elections) in the "Declaration of Principles." Women activists had been diligently fighting for the right to vote for forty years before that document was written. And it was not until sixteen years after the Declaration that women were granted the right to vote by a Constitutional amendment.

The campaign for women's suffrage had been initiated in 1848 at a women's rights convention in Seneca Falls, New York. In addition to voting rights, the convention agenda included women's property rights, the right of women to enroll in institutions of higher learning, and the right of women to earn pay equal to that of men for equal work.

In the 1850s and early 1860s the women's rights movement foundered as activists turned their efforts toward the abolition (outlawing) of slavery. After the Civil War (1861–1865) and the emancipation of the slaves, the question of voting rights rose again. Women's advocates and abolitionists (people who worked for the immediate termination of

> "We demand that all constitutional and legal barriers shall be removed which deny to women any individual right or personal freedom which is granted to men."

Susan B. Anthony (right) and Elizabeth Cady Stanton formed the National Woman Suffrage Association (NWSA) in 1869. The NWSA's goal was the passage of a Constitutional amendment granting women the right to vote. *Reproduced by permission of the Library of Congress.*

slavery) pushed for "universal suffrage"—the granting of voting rights to both freed slaves and women.

Despite the efforts of women's rights activists, the postwar amendments that gave rights to blacks did not enfranchise (give the vote to) women. The Fourteenth Amendment, ratified in 1868, guaranteed all citizens (interpreted by the courts to mean "all male citizens") equal protection under the laws. The Fifteenth Amendment, ratified in 1870, granted black males the right to vote (that amendment was subsequently undermined by a series of racist laws).

Just prior to the ratification of the Fifteenth Amendment, a split developed within in the women's suffrage movement. In one camp were women who believed that too much attention was being focused on the right of black men to vote, at the expense of women's suffrage. In the other camp were women who prioritized securing the black male vote and felt that women should be patient regarding their own rights. Members of the former camp formed the National Woman Suffrage Association (NWSA); members of the latter camp formed the American Woman Suffrage Association (AWSA).

With author Julia Ward Howe, Lucy Stone founded the American Woman Suffrage Association.
Reproduced by permission of Archive Photos.

The NWSA was led by Susan B. Anthony (1820–1906), considered the movement's best organizer, and Elizabeth Cady Stanton (1815–1092), considered the movement's leading philosopher and writer. The goal of the NWSA was the passage of a constitutional amendment granting women the right to vote. The NWSA, which was considered more radical than the AWSA, did not admit men and even criticized the churches for their sexist teachings.

The AWSA was founded by well-known orator Lucy Stone (1818–1893) and author Julia Ward Howe (1819–1910). The women chose a man as president of their organization, the Reverend Henry Ward Beecher. The strategy of the AWSA was to lobby for women's suffrage on a state-by-state basis.

The NWSA and the AWSA put aside their differences in 1890 and formed a single organization—the National American Woman Suffrage Association (NAWSA). Stanton became the group's first president; Anthony was elected to be the group's second president in 1892.

The NAWSA worked steadily over the next twenty years for the passage of a constitutional amendment granting women's suffrage. The organization circulated petitions, held demonstrations, and lobbied state and federal lawmakers. In 1904, when the "Declaration of Principles" was written, the NAWSA was under the leadership of gifted organizer Carrie Chapman Catt (1859–1947).

Things to remember while reading "Women Should Have the Right to Vote":

- The American Revolution, also called the Seven Years' War or the War of the Revolution, took place from 1775 to 1781. At the root of the rebellion was Great Britain's economic exploitation of the American colonies. The colonists' charge of "taxation without representation" meant that the colonists were being taxed by Great Britain without having a voice in the policies affecting them. Woman suffragists later claimed that women, with no right to vote, were being subjected to a U.S. government policy of "taxation without representation."

- Prior to the 1860s, women in the United States had no property rights. A woman's belongings, her inheritance, and even her children were legally the property of her husband or, if she was unmarried, her father. New York state passed the nation's first Married Woman's Property Act in 1860, giving every married woman control over her possessions and joint-guardianship of her children with her husband. Several other state legislatures passed similar laws over the following decade.

- The United States took control of Puerto Rico and the Philippines in 1898 during the Spanish-American War; the United States acquired Hawaii as a territory in 1900. In those U.S. territories or possessions, as in the United States, women were denied the right to vote. In the Declaration of Principles, the NAWSA also demanded suffrage for "the women of our foreign possessions."

"Women Should Have the Right to Vote "

When our forefathers gained the victory in a seven years' war to establish the principle that representation should go hand in hand with taxation, they marked a new epoch in the history of man; but though our foremothers bore an equal part in that long conflict its triumph brought to them no added rights and through all the following century and a quarter, taxation without representation has been continuously imposed on women by as great tyranny as **King George** exercised over the American colonists.

So long as no married woman was permitted to own property and all women were barred from the money-making occupations this discrimination did not seem so **invidious**; but to-day the situation is without a parallel. The women of the United States now pay taxes on real and personal estate valued at billions of dollars. In a number of individual States their holdings amount to many millions. Everywhere they are accumulating property. In hundreds of places they form one-third of the taxpayers, with the number constantly increasing, and yet they are absolutely without representation in the affairs of the nation, of the State, even of the community in which they live and pay taxes. We enter our protest against this injustice and we demand that the immortal principles established by the War of the Revolution shall be applied equally to women and men citizens.

Half the Citizenry Has No Voice

As our new republic passed into a higher stage of development the gross inequality became apparent of giving representation to capital and denying it to labor; therefore the right of suffrage was extended to the workingman. Now we demand for the 4,000,000 wage-earning women of our country the same protection of the ballot as is possessed by the wage-earning men.

The founders took an even broader view of human rights when they declared that government could justly derive its powers only from the consent of the governed, and for 125 years this grand assertion was regarded as a corner-stone of the republic, with scarcely a recognition of the fact that one-half of the citizens were as completely governed without their consent as were the people of any **absolute monarchy** in existence. It was only when our government was extended over alien

King George: George III; full name, George William Frederick (1738–1820); king of England during the American Revolution (1775–81).

Invidious: Causing resentment.

Absolute monarchy: A government headed by a king that is not limited by laws or a constitution.

"When Woman Gets Her Rights, Man Will Be Right"

Sojourner Truth (1797–1883) was born a slave in Ulster County, New York. After gaining her freedom in 1826, Truth became an abolitionist, a women's rights advocate, and a preacher. She rose to fame as a dynamic lecturer at a time when African Americans and women typically lived on the margins of society.

Following the emancipation of the slaves, Truth joined the fight for women's suffrage. As an uneducated person, an African American, and a former slave, Truth brought a unique perspective to the mainly white and educated ranks of the women's rights movement.

In Truth's "When Woman Gets Her Rights, Man Will be Right" speech—as in many of her speeches—Truth refers to the members of the audience as "chil'n," or children. What follows is an excerpt:

My Friends, I am rejoiced that you are glad, but I don't know how you will feel when I get through. I come from another field—the country of the slave. They have got their rights—so much good luck. Now what is to be done about it? I feel that I have got as much responsibility as anybody else. I have as good rights as anybody. There is a great stir about colored men getting their rights, but not a word about the colored women; and if colored men get their rights, and not colored women get theirs, there will be a bad time about it. So I am for keeping the thing going while things are stirring; because if we wait till it is still, it will take a great while to get it going again. White women are a great deal smarter and know more than colored women, while colored women do not know scarcely anything. They go out washing, which is about as high as a colored woman gets, and their men go about idle, strutting up and down; and when the women come home, they ask for their money and take it all, and then scold because there is no food. I want you to consider that, chil'n. I want women to

races in foreign countries that our people awoke to the meaning of the principles of the Declaration of Independence. In response to its provisions, the Congress of the United States hastened to invest with the power of consent the men of this new territory, but committed the flagrant injustice of withholding it from the women. We demand that the ballot shall be extended to the women of our foreign possessions on the same terms as to the men. Furthermore, we demand that the women of the United States shall no longer suffer the degradation of being held not so competent to exercise the suffrage as a Filipino, a Hawaiian or a Porto [sic] Rican man.

The remaining Territories within the United States are insisting upon admission into the Union on the ground that their citizens desire

Sojourner Truth. *Reproduced by permission of the National Portrait Gallery.*

have their rights. In the courts women have no right, no voice; nobody speaks for them.... I suppose I am about the only colored woman that goes about to speak for the rights of the colored woman, I want to keep the thing stirring, now that the ice is broken.... I know that it is hard for one who has held the reins for so long to give up; it cuts like a knife. It will feel all better when it closes up again....

I know that it is hard for men to give up entirely. They must run in the old track. I was amused how men speak up for one another. They cannot bear that a woman should say anything about the man, but they will stand here and take up the time in man's cause.... Men have got their rights, and women has not got their rights. That is the trouble. When woman gets her rights man will be right. How beautiful that will be. Then it will be peace on earth and good will to men.... The great fight was to keep the rights of the poor colored people. That made a great battle. And now I hope that this will be the last battle that will be in the world. Let us finish up so that there be no more fighting.

Excerpt from Worlds of Fire: An Anthology of African-American Feminist Thought, *edited by Beverly Guy-Sheftall. The New Press, 1995..*

"the right to select their own governing officials, choose their own judges, name those who are to make their laws and levy, collect, and disburse their taxes." These are just and commendable desires but we demand that their women shall have full recognition as citizens when these Territories are admitted and that their constitutions shall secure to women precisely the same rights as to men.

When our government was founded the **rudiments** of education were thought sufficient for women, since their entire time was absorbed in the multitude of household duties. Now the number of girls graduated by the high schools greatly exceeds the number of boys in every State and the percentage of women students in the colleges is vastly larger than that of men. Meantime most of the domes-

Rudiments: The basics or first principles of a subject.

tic industries have been taken from the home to the factory and hundreds of thousands of women have followed them there, while the more highly trained have entered the professions and other avenues of skilled labor. We demand that under this new régime, and in view of these changed conditions in which she is so important a factor woman shall have a voice and a vote in the solution of their innumerable problems.

Other Injustices

The laws of practically every State provide that the husband shall select the place of residence for the family, and if the wife refuse to abide by his choice she forfeits her right to support and her refusal shall be regarded as desertion. We protest against the recent decision of the courts which has added to this injustice by requiring the wife also to accept for herself the citizenship preferred by her husband, thus compelling a woman born in the United States to lose her nationality if her husband choose to declare his allegiance to a foreign country.

As women form two-thirds of the church membership of the entire nation; as they constitute but one-eleventh of the convicted criminals; as they are rapidly becoming the educated class and as the salvation of our government depends upon a moral, law-abiding, educated electorate, we demand for the sake of its integrity and permanence that women be made a part of its voting body.

In brief, we demand that all constitutional and legal barriers shall be removed which deny to women any individual right or personal freedom which is granted to men. This we ask in the name of a democratic and a republican government, which, its constitution declares, was formed "to establish justice and secure the blessings of liberty." (Wekesser, pp. 18–20)

What happened next...

Eighteen-sixty-nine marked the first year in which a women's suffrage bill was introduced into the House of Representatives. Not surprisingly, the bill failed. It was not until 1919—after countless picket lines in front of the White House, arrests of many suffragists, and even hunger strikes—that the proposed constitutional amendment won congressional approval. The following year the amendment won ratification from the necessary thirty-six states (ratification by three-fourths of all states is necessary for the adoption of any Constitutional amendment). By that time, a majority of states had already granted women the right to vote.

The Nineteenth Amendment reads, in its entirety: "The right of citizens of the United States to vote shall not be denied or abridged by the United States or by any State on account of sex. Congress shall have power to enforce this article by appropriate legislation."

Did you know...

- In 1872 Susan B. Anthony was arrested for voting in a presidential election in Rochester, New York, and fined $100. Anthony refused to pay the fine, calling it an "unjust penalty."

- Lucy Stone pioneered the practice of women keeping their birth names after marriage in 1855, when she refused to change her name upon marrying Henry B. Blackwell.

- A report by the Washington, D.C.-based Institute for Women's Policy published in 1999—almost eighty years after women were given the right to vote—revealed that a woman, on average, earns only 74 cents for every dollar earned by a man.

For More Information See

Books

Harper, Ida Husted, ed. "Declaration of Principles," in *The History of Woman Suffrage*. Vol. 5, appendix to chapter 4. New York: American Woman Suffrage Association, 1992.

Sources

Books

McElroy, Lorie Jenkins, ed. *Women's Voices*. Detroit: U•X•L, 1997.

Rhode, Deborah L. "Nineteenth Amendment," in *Civil Rights and Equality*. Edited by Leonard W. Levy, Kenneth L. Karst, and Dennis J. Mahoney. New York: MacMillan, 1989.

Schmittroth, Linda, and Mary Reilly McCall, eds. *Women's Almanac.* Detroit: U•X•L, 1997.

Sinclair, Barbara. *The Women's Movement: Political, Socioeconomic and Psychological Issues.* New York: Harper and Row Publishers, 1975.

Weisberg, Barbara. *Susan B. Anthony.* New York: Chelsea House, 1988.

Wekesser, Carol, ed. "Women Should Have the Right to Vote," in *Feminism: Opposing Viewpoints.* San Diego, CA: Greenhaven Press, Inc., 1995, pp. 18–20.

Periodicals

Kellogg, Sarah. "Women's Pay Gap Hurting Families, Union Study Finds." *The Ann Arbor News.* February 25, 1999: C5.

Gay and Lesbian Rights

Statements of support by Paul Wellstone, Joseph E. Lowery, Jesse Jackson, and Maxine Waters

Excerpts from Gay and Lesbian Rights: A Reference Handbook
Published in 1994

The movement for gay and lesbian rights in the United States came of age in the 1960s. Over the last thirty years gay individuals in ever larger numbers have been openly asserting their homosexuality (sexual desire or behavior exhibited between persons of the same sex. Heterosexuality is sexual desire or behavior exhibited between persons of the opposite sex.) In 1975 the American Psychiatric Association advanced the cause of gay rights when it dispelled the long-held myth that homosexuality is a mental disorder. Sixty-four percent of people interviewed in an October 1998 *Time Magazine*/CNN poll claimed to be accepting of homosexuals (this represents a dramatic rise over the 35 percent of interviewees who answered affirmatively in a 1978 poll).

Respect for the rights of gay men and lesbians today, however, is by no means universal. While some states and localities have statutes defending the civil rights of lesbians and gay men, there are statutes on the books denying those rights in other locations. On the question of marriage, the door has been shut to gay couples. At present no state in the union allows same-sex marriages and in 1996 the federal gov-

> "Lesbians and gay men come from every part of society and from every stripe of the rainbow, and are an integral part of the quilt that is America."
>
> *Reverend Jesse Jackson*

ernment, with the passage of the Defense of Marriage Act, denied homosexuals the right to marry.

Numerous politicians, social activists, and religious leaders have entered both sides of the debate over gay and lesbian rights. Reproduced here are statements by four prominent civic leaders in favor of gay and lesbian rights.

Gay rights demonstrators in New York City.
Photograph by Betty Lane. Reproduced by permission of Photo Researchers, Inc.

Things to remember while reading the statements in support of gay and lesbian rights:

- In 1974 Representative Bella Abzug of New York introduced into Congress the Gay and Lesbian Civil Rights Bill—a federal statute that would have banned discrimination against lesbians and gay men in a variety of arenas. The bill was voted down in 1974, as it has been in several subsequent sessions of Congress.

- Prior to 1993, gay men and lesbians were prohibited from serving in the U.S. armed forces. Suspicion of a service-member's homosexuality was grounds for that individual's discharge. In July 1993 the secretary of defense, under the direction of President Bill Clinton, issued a new policy regarding gays in the military. Commonly known as "Don't Ask, Don't Tell" the policy stated that a service-member could not be expelled merely on suspicion of his or her homosexuality. An individual could be discharged, however, if that individual revealed that he or she was gay. In January 1999, a report released by the Defense Department indicated that in the years since the implementation of the "Don't Ask, Don't Tell" policy the number of gay men and lesbians discharged from the armed services had risen steadily. There were nearly twice the number of discharges in 1998 as there were in 1992—the year before the new policy took effect.

Marchers at the 1993
Gay Rights March
on Washington.
*Reproduced by permission
of Cathy Cade.*

Remarks at the Gay Rights March on Washington, June 1993

by Senator Paul Wellstone

Paul Wellstone was first elected to the U.S. Senate from Minnesota in 1990, and was reelected in 1996. Prior to becoming a senator Wellstone spent several years as a community organizer and a college professor. Wellstone, a Democrat, works for universal health care, anti-poverty measures, improved public education, and job training. Wellstone was the only senator to speak at the 1993 Gay Rights March on Washington. His remarks were originally printed in The Advocate, *June 15, 1993.*

I come here as a United States senator from Minnesota. I have always said to my wife, Sheila, and our children that leadership is not about appealing to the hatred or the fear or the frustrations of people; leadership is about inspiring people to be their own best selves.

And as a United States senator, I want you to know that I support this rally for human rights and civil rights for all people, regardless of sexual orientation.

I am an American Jew, and even though we faced centuries of discrimination, it could never quench the fire of human dignity. And so it was with the people of color in our civil rights movement; regardless of the hatred, regardless of the discrimination, the fire of human dignity could never be put out. And it will be human dignity that will sustain this movement, and we will make sure that in the United States of America, we will put an end to discrimination on the basis of sexual orientation and we'll have human rights and dignity for each and every citizen throughout our country.

I want to tell each and every one of you that I want to be accountable, and I want you to know that as a United States senator—and I'm proud to be a senator—I believe that you will have support from other senators and representatives, and I believe you will have the support of the president.

Keep on marching, keep on fighting. Keep on marching, keep on fighting. Lobby, write letters, be a voice so we can make the United States of America all that she can be. I thank you very much.

Joseph E. Lowery
Reproduced by permission of AP/Wide World Photos.

Letter to the editor
by Reverend Joseph E. Lowery

Joseph Lowery (1924–) is president of the Southern Christian Leadership Conference (SCLC). The SCLC is a civil rights organization of African American clergy, founded in 1957 by Martin Luther King Jr. (1929–1968). Lowery served as the organization's first vice president and a top aide to King. During Lowery's presidency, the SCLC has embraced a range of issues regarding social and economic justice and human rights. Lowery's letter first appeared in the Bay Area Reporter, *July 8, 1993.*

It would be ridiculously and drastically inconsistent for us to support the denial of lesbians and gays to equal opportunity and equal access to serve their country in the military. Lesbians and gays have as much right to serve their country and fight and die for their country as anyone else.

Citizens of diverse sexual orientation have served in the military since its beginning and with distinction.

This nation cannot deny any of its citizens the right to serve their government solely because some do not approve of sexual orientation. How could we survive as a nation if we granted civil/human rights based on the whimsical likes and dislikes of other citizens?

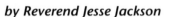

Statement regarding gay and lesbian rights

by Reverend Jesse Jackson

Jesse Jackson (1941–) served as an aide to Martin Luther King Jr. from 1966 to 1968. In 1971 he founded the Chicago-based economic justice organization PUSH (for People United to Serve Humanity). The only African American to have run for United States president, Jackson vied unsuccessfully for the Democratic presidential nomination in both 1984 and 1988. Jackson remains an activist in the arenas of anti-discrimination, workers' rights, and voter registration. Jackson's statement originally appeared in Who Supports the Gay and Lesbian Rights Movement?, *published by the National Gay and Lesbian Task Force in 1990.*

Jesse Jackson.
Reproduced by permission of the Library of Congress.

Lesbians and gay men come from every part of society and from every stripe of the rainbow, and are an integral part of the quilt that is America. They are Black, Latino, Catholic, Jew, farmers, unemployed, homeless, students and parents. As citizens of this great country, lesbians and gay men must be afforded all the rights the Constitution provides.

We support the current Lesbian and Gay Civil Rights Bill in the U.S. Congress, which calls for an end to discrimination based on sexual orientation. We support the implementation of a Presidential Order banning anti-gay discrimination in the federal government and the military.

Maxine Waters.
Reproduced by permission of AP/Wide World Photos.

Statement regarding gay and lesbian rights

by Congresswoman Maxine Waters

*Maxine Waters (1938–) was first elected to the U.S. House of Representatives as a Democrat from California in 1990; she has subsequently been re-elected four times. Prior to her entry into national politics, Waters served as a member of the California State Assembly for fourteen years. On both state and national levels, Waters has championed the needs of poor people, black and Latino youth, and the environment. She is an outspoken opponent of police brutality and a proponent of **affirmative action** programs.*

Waters's statement first appeared in Who Supports the Gay and Lesbian Rights Movement?, *published by the National Gay and Lesbian Task Force in 1990.*

All human beings have a fundamental right to privacy and to define their own sexuality. Attempts by the state ·to restrict these rights are among the most unfair and unjustified actions it can take. Unfortunately, lesbians and gay men must still fight for their most basic rights. It is a disgrace that this debate is even necessary. Our government has continually denied lesbians and gay men labor rights, housing rights, health care rights—indeed civil rights. Thus, it is up to the people, once again, to force the government to accept the rights of lesbians and gay men. (Newton, pp. 94–95, 98–99)

What happened next...

While gay rights activists have achieved many victories over the last few decades, they have experienced a handful of setbacks in recent years. For instance, ten states and dozens of cities have adopted antidiscrimination measures that protect the rights of lesbians and gay men in housing, employment, and other areas. In February 1998, however, Maine residents voted to

Affirmative action: A set of programs, primarily in education and employment, that give preferential treatment to racial minorities and women.

overturn a 1997 state law protecting lesbians and gay men from discrimination in employment, housing, credit, and public accommodations. And in 1993, Cincinnati voters approved a charter amendment that denies discrimination protection to gay men and lesbians. (The Supreme Court, in an October 1998 ruling, upheld the validity of the Cincinnati statute.)

A serious, ongoing problem confronting gay men and lesbians is violence directed against them. Federal Bureau of Information (FBI) statistics indicate that in 1995 there were 1,019 incidents of anti-gay violence nationwide. (The actual number was probably much higher, given that the majority of incidents of anti-gay violence go unreported). According to the National Coalition of Anti-Violence Programs, an organization that monitors anti-gay violence, violent crimes against gay men and lesbians increased 6 percent in 1996 over the previous year. The FBI reported 1,102 hate crimes against lesbians and gay men in 1997.

A handful of anti-gay attacks in recent years have received national attention. One of the most brutal cases was the beating death of Matthew Shepard in Laramie, Wyoming, in October 1998. Shepard, a twenty-one-year-old gay student at the University of Wyoming, was beaten unconscious by two high school dropouts from Laramie. The assailants tied Shepard to a fencepost in near-freezing temperatures and left him to die.

Anti-gay violence made headlines again in February 1999. Two men known for their racist and antihomosexual views beat and burned to death Billy Jack Gaither, a thirty-nine-year-old textile worker, in Sylacauga, Alabama.

Did you know...

- On November 3, 1998, voters in both Hawaii and Alaska supported referenda to alter their state constitutions to ban same-sex marriages. Prior to those votes, gay activists had reason for optimism regarding their rights to marry in those states. In the mid 1990s, the right of gay couples to wed had been upheld by the state supreme court of Hawaii and a superior court judge in Alaska.

- Senate majority leader Trent Lott is among the most strident opponents of gay rights on Capitol Hill. Lott stated that he considers homosexuality a sin during a June 1998 taping of *The Armstrong Williams Show*. "You should try to show them," said Lott, in reference to gay men and lesbians, "a way to deal with that problem, just like alcohol ... or sex addiction ... or kleptomaniacs."

- In December 1998 the American Psychiatric Association renounced the use of therapy aimed at converting gay individuals into heterosexuals, claiming that such therapy may produce depression or self-destructive behavior in its subjects.

For More Information See

Books

Who Supports the Gay and Lesbian Rights Movement? Washington, D.C.: National Gay and Lesbian Task Force, 1990.

Sources

Books

Adam, Barry D. *The Rise of a Gay and Lesbian Movement.* Boston: Twayne Publishers, 1987.

African American Biography. Vol. 3. Detroit: U•X•L, 1994, pp. 482–84.

Katz, Jonathan. *Gay American History: Lesbians and Gay Men in the U.S.A.* New York: Harper & Row Publishers, 1976.

Newton, David E., ed. *Gay and Lesbian Rights: A Reference Handbook.* Santa Barbara, CA: ABC-CLIO, 1994.

Smith, Sande, ed. *Who's Who in African American History.* New York: Smithmark, 1994, p. 78.

Periodicals

Cloud, John. "For Better or Worse: In Hawaii, a Showdown Over Marriage Tests the Limits of Gay Activism." *Time.* October 26, 1998: 43–44.

Conniff, Ruth. "President Wellstone? A Liberal Populist Considers a Run." *The Nation.* May 18, 1998: 11–16.

"FBI: Race is Top Hate-Crime Motive." *The Ann Arbor News.* January 22, 1999: A7

Ireland, Doug. "Maine's Gay Retreat." *The Nation.* March 9, 1998: 6.

Lacayo, Richard. "The New Gay Struggle." *Time.* October 26, 1998: 32–36.

Meyers, Steven Lee. "Military Discharges for Homosexuality Double in Five Years." *New York Times*. January 23, 1999.

"Senator Leader Calls Homosexuality a Problem Like 'Kleptomaniacs.'" Associated Press. June 16, 1998: A4.

"Suspect in Killing of Gay Man Wanted to be a Skinhead." *The Ann Arbor News*. March 6, 1999: A3.

Weller, Robert. "Psychiatrists Reject 'Conversion' of Gays." *The Ann Arbor News*. December 13, 1998: A8.

Web Sites

Congresswoman Maxine Waters. National School Network. [Online] Available http://nsn.bbn.com/community/bl_hist/waters_bio.shtml (last accessed March 19, 1999).

Federal Bureau of Investigation. "Uniform Crime Reports: Hate Crime 1995." [Online] Available http://www.fbi.gov.ucr/hatecm.htm#bias (last accessed December 3, 1998).

Voter Information Services. "VIS Ratings for Representatives of California." [Online] Available. http://world.std.com/~voteinfo/ascii_reports/CA/35.html (last accessed March 19, 1999).

American Coalition of Citizens with Disabilities

Disabled Peoples' Bill of Rights
Excerpt from *Disabled People as Second-Class Citizens*
Published in 1982

There are more than 49 million people with disabilities in the United States today. Disability is legally defined as any physical or mental condition that restricts one or more of an individual's major life activities. Examples of disabilities are blindness, deafness, disuse of one or more limbs, mental illness, and HIV-positive status. (HIV, which stands for human immunodeficiency virus, is the agent that causes AIDS—acquired immunodeficiency syndrome.)

People with disabilities have been, and continue to be, victimized by discrimination in American society. For example, there is housing segregation (the placement of people with disabilities in institutions) and educational segregation (the placement of students with disabilities in "special education" classrooms). People with disabilities are typically excluded from many types of employment and are often excluded—due to physical barriers—from some forms of public transportation and other public accommodations.

Having endured unfair treatment for centuries, people with disabilities lag behind the general population in terms of income, level of educational attainment, and employment

"Because people with disabilities have consistently been denied the right to fully participate in society as free and equal members, it is important to state and affirm these rights. All people should be able to enjoy these rights, regardless of race, creed, color, sex, religion, or disability."

Disabled protesters picket the Federal Aviation Administration (FAA) in July 1978. At issue was an FAA regulation that forbade blind persons from bringing their canes on commercial airline flights. *Reproduced by permission of AP/Wide World Photos.*

rates. Due to a lack of understanding of disabilities, members of the general public routinely underestimate the capabilities of individuals with disabilities.

There were several federal and state statutes passed in the 1960s, 1970s, and 1980s, outlawing various forms of discrimination against people with disabilities. This network of laws, however, did not offer people with disabilities complete protection. Discrimination by privately owned businesses, for example, was not outlawed. It was not until the passage of the Americans with Disabilities Act in 1990 that the rights of people with disabilities were fully guaranteed by law.

Advances in the rights of people with disabilities in the past three decades have only come about through the concerted efforts of disability rights activists. The disability rights movement got its start in Berkeley, California, in the mid-1960s, when disabled college students demanded access to university and city facilities. The movement took on a national scope with the founding of the Center for Independent Living—an agency run by and for persons with disabilities, now with chapters in more than 400 cities—in 1972.

Things to remember while reading the "Disabled Peoples' Bill of Rights":

- At the time this document was written, people with disabilities had few guarantees of civil rights. A 1986 poll by Lou Harris and Associates, entitled "Bringing Disabled Americans into the Mainstream," concluded the following: "By almost any definition, Americans with disabilities are uniquely underprivileged and disadvantaged. They are much poorer, much less well educated and have much less social life, have fewer amenities and have a lower level of self-satisfaction than other Americans."

Disabled Peoples' Bill of Rights

Preamble

We believe that all people should enjoy certain rights. Because people with disabilities have consistently been denied the right to fully participate in society as free and equal members, it is important to state and affirm these rights. All people should be able to enjoy these rights, regardless of race, creed, color, sex, religion, or disability.

1. *The right to live independent, active, and full lives.*

2. *The right to the equipment, assistance, and support services necessary for full productivity, provided in a way that promotes dignity and independence.*

3. *The right to an adequate income or wage, substantial enough to provide food, clothing, shelter, and other necessities of life.*

4. *The right to accessible, integrated, convenient, and affordable housing.*

5. *The right to quality physical and mental health care.*

6. *The right to training and employment without prejudice or* **stereotype.**

7. *The right to accessible transportation and freedom of movement.*

8. *The right to bear or adopt and raise children and have a family.*

9. *The right to a free and appropriate public education.*

10. *The right to participate in and benefit from entertainment and recreation.*

11. *The right of equal access to and use of all businesses, facilities, and activities in the community.*

12. *The right to communicate freely with all fellow citizens and those who provide services.*

13. *The right to a barrier free environment.*

14. *The right to legal representation and to full protection of all legal rights.*

15. *The right to determine one's own future and make one's own life choices.*

16. *The right of full access to all voting processes. (Eisenberg et al., pp. 292–93)*

Stereotype: A widely held idea or image of someone, usually based on ignorance or prejudice.

What happened next...

The bleak state of civil rights for people with disabilities was brightened in 1990 with the passage of the Americans with Disabilities Act (ADA). The ADA is a comprehensive series of guarantees of equal treatment for people with disabilities. It bans discrimination against people with disabilities in employment, government-run programs and services, public accommodations (such as hotels, restaurants, and movie theaters), and telecommunications.

The legislative protections offered by the ADA, together with improved services and new technologies, have vastly increased the opportunities for people with disabilities to lead independent, productive lives.

Did you know...

- The World Institute on Disability (WID) was begun with funds from a "genius award," worth $225,000, granted to disability rights activist Ed Roberts (1939–1995).

- The first major piece of federal legislation assisting people with disabilities, ratified in 1968, was the Architectural Barriers Act (ABA). The ABA required that buildings financed or leased by the federal government be handicapped-accessible.

Sources

Books

Eisenberg, Myron G., Cynthia Griggins, and Richard J. Duval, eds. *Disabled People as Second-Class Citizens.* New York: Springer Publishing Company, 1982, pp. 292–93.

Harrison, Maureen, and Steve Gilbert, eds. *The Americans with Disabilities Act Handbook.* Beverly Hills, CA: Excellent Books, 1992.

Kent, Deborah, and Kathryn A. Quinlan. *Extraordinary People with Disabilities.* New York: Children's Press, 1996, pp. 127–132.

Sigler, Jay A., ed. *Civil Rights in America: 1500 to the Present.* Detroit: Gale, 1998.

Thompson-Hoffman, Susan, and Inez Fitzgerald Storck, eds. *Disability in the United States: A Portrait From National Data.* New York: Springer Publishing Company, 1991.

West, Jane, ed. *Implementing the Americans with Disabilities Act.* Cambridge, MA: Blackwell Publishers, Inc., 1996.

Pamphlets

Americans with Disabilities Act of 1990. Alexandria, VA: National Mental Health Association, 1991.

Judith Heumann

Since June 1993 Judith Heumann has served as the Clinton Administration's Assistant Secretary for Special Education and Rehabilitative Services. Heumann, who is paralyzed from the waist down, oversees the efforts of 350 employees at three agencies: the Office of Special Education Programs; the Rehabilitation Services Administration; and the National Institute on Disability and Rehabilitation Research. These agencies provide services to disabled individuals throughout the United States.

Heumann graduated from Long Island University in 1969. Six years later she complete a master's degree in public health administration at the University of California, Berkeley. Before assuming her current post, Heumann served for ten years as vice president of the World Institute on Disability (WID). The WID, of which Heumann was a cofounder, is an Oakland-based international public policy organization that sponsors research into disability issues and promotes the integration of people with disabilities into every aspect of society.

President's Committee on Employment of People with Disabilities. *Americans with Disabilities Act in Brief*. Washington, D.C.: GPO, 1992.

U.S. Equal Employment Opportunity Commission. *The Americans with Disabilities Act: Questions and Answers*. Washington, D.C.: GPO, 1992.

Web Sites

Center for Independent Living. [Online] Available http://www.cilberkeley.org/ (last accessed April 12, 1999).

Text Credits

The editors wish to thank the copyright holders of the excerpted documents included in this volume and the permissions managers of many book and magazine publishing companies for assisting us in securing reproduction rights. What follows is a list of the copyright holders who have granted us permission to reproduce material for *American Civil Rights: Primary Sources*. Every effort has been made to trace copyright; if omissions have been made, please contact the publisher.

Cantarow, Ellen. From *Moving the Mountain*. Feminist Press, 1980. Copyright © 1980 by The Feminist Press, Box 334, Old Westbury, New York 11568. All rights reserved. Reproduced by permission.

Clark, Kenneth B. From *Prejudice and Your Child*. Beacon Press, 1951. Copyright © 1955 by Beacon Press, Inc., 1963 by Beacon Press. Renewed 1983 by Kenneth B. Clark. Reproduced by permission.

Eisenberg, Myron G., Cynthia Griggins, and Richard J. Duval, eds. From appendix "Disabled Peoples' Bill of

Newton, David. From *Gay and Lesbian Rights: A Reference Handbook*. ABC-Clio, Inc., 1994. Copyright © 1994 Instructional Horizons, Inc. All rights reserved. Reproduced by permission.

Vera Cruz, Philip. "Sour Grapes: A Symbol of Oppression," published in *GIRDA*. November 1970.

Index

Bold type indicates
main documents and
speaker profiles.

**Illustrations are marked
by (ill.).**